THE ELEPHANT AND MY JEWISH PROBLEM

THE
ELEPHANT
AND
MY JEWISH
PROBLEM

SELECTED STORIES
AND JOURNALS
1957–1987

HUGH
NISSENSON

PERENNIAL LIBRARY

An Edward Burlingame Book

Harper & Row, Publishers, New York

Grand Rapids, Philadelphia, St. Louis, San Francisco

London, Singapore, Sydney, Tokyo, Toronto

For Elbert Lenrow and Shy Raz

CONTENTS

THE ELEPHANT AND MY JEWISH PROBLEM

THE BLESSING

When Rabbi Levinsky finally left, it was late in the afternoon. Yitshaak went out onto the balcony to watch the old man going home. His black coat flapped about his knees as he walked up the hill. The road was lined by eucalyptus trees. From time to time the old man paused to catch his breath. Even on the balcony, the air was stifling, redolent of plaster and the exhaust fumes of cars. The long tapering leaves of the trees, shaped like knife blades, were covered with dust. The heated air shimmered above the red-tiled roofs of the houses on top of the hill. Beyond them, to the west, beyond the highway to Haifa, and shining between the gaps in the sand dunes, the inert Mediterranean reflected the pale-blue sky.

On the crest of the hill, Levinsky looked back. Yitshaak drew away from the railing, but it was too late; the old man had seen him, and with a gesture that was unmistakable in spite of the distance, he reproved him again with a shake of his head. Then he went on. The road turned left. Yitshaak watched until he was hidden by the row of whitewashed houses and the dusty trees.

Standing there, facing the road, Yitshaak could see the grammar school for the children of the neighborhood. It was here that his son had been enrolled in the third grade before he had been taken ill. Yitshaak put his hand to his forehead, shielding his eyes from the sun, in an effort to see into the classroom where the boy had studied. It was on the first floor, north, in the corner of the building. The window was dark.

He took a deep breath. Since three-thirty, when he had returned home from the hospital at Petach Tikva, he had longed only to be left alone with his wife, Nira, who had taken to her bed as soon as she had heard the news. Now, with Levinsky gone, he was frightened at the thought of it. He was grateful that Esther, her aunt, was with her. Not that it really made any difference; he was going to have to tell them both what he had decided. In a way, Esther was responsible. He thought back to earlier in the afternoon and pictured her standing in the doorway when she had first heard about the boy, with one plump arm raised, and those disquieting eyes becoming suddenly brilliant with tears. His gaze returned to the school. A little yellow Arab dog, casting an enormous shadow in the light of the declining sun, was crossing the yard with its nose to the ground.

"Yitshaak?"

It was Esther from the living room. "Yitshaak? Yitshaak, where are you?" He gave himself a moment more—until the dog reached the corner of the building, and then went to face her in the open door.

"There you are. Where is he? Levinsky's gone?"

"A few minutes ago."

"Without saying goodbye?"

Her eyes were pale blue, clear and untroubled, like a child's. This afternoon was the first time he had ever seen her cry. She had been in the country for twelve years, the only member of her immediate family to survive the concentration camps. Belsen, a trek across the Alps in winter and on foot, a year's internment on Cyprus, and now the shabby rented room in Ramat Gan where she lived alone, without complaint, and supported herself as a dressmaker's assistant—her quiet eyes revealed nothing of what she had seen.

"What about tomorrow?" she asked. "What time does the service start?"

"Early. Eight-thirty."

"That's a good idea. The earlier the better. We'll get Nira back here before it gets too hot."

"I guess so."

"From Petach Tikva? Why not? It won't take more than a half hour to get home. If the service starts promptly at eight-thirty, we'll be back here by eleven at the latest. What about the hired cars?"

"What about them?"

"How many are you going to have?"

"One. Why?"

"I thought so. That's not enough. That's only enough for the four of us—Levinsky, you, me, and Nira. What about Zvi and the Rosens?" They were clerks with whom Yitshaak worked in the safe-deposit department of the bank on Allenby Road.

"Zvi'll drive himself," he said.

"Has he got a car?"

"A Jeep."

"Wonderful. I didn't know. Who else? How about Lani? What's her name? You know. Nira's friend from school. Oh, you know who I mean. The girl who married that doctor in Natanya."

"Goldman."

"That's the one."

"They're away," Yitshaak said. "They went away on vacation."

"Where?"

"I don't know. Nira may know."

"She's sleeping. You can ask her when she gets up. We'll send them a telegram. Would you like me to call the others?"

"If you like."

"I'll call them from the pharmacy when I go shopping. Oh. That reminds me. Something else. It's important. I almost forgot."

"What?"

"If they all go to the cemetery, we'll have to invite them back here afterward for something to eat."

"Yes," said Yitshaak. "I remember. The meal of condolence." It seemed so remote; all of the random memories of his religious upbringing seemed now to belong to another life; the dark Polish synagogue on Dizengoff Road with its slippery floor, the candles and fish on Friday night, the red velvet *tallis* bag that his father had given him on his thirteenth birthday. . .

"We'll have to give them eggs or lentils to begin with," Esther said. "That's required. After that, you can have whatever you like; meat if you want. I thought maybe I'd make veal cutlets."

He shrugged; she chattered on, now and again dabbing at the sweat on her upper lip.

"What is it?" she asked. "Is anything the matter?"

"No, no, go on. I'm listening," he said, coming into the room at last and sitting himself down on the sofa with his hands on his knees.

"Did he tell you I knew his wife?"

"Who?"

"Levinsky."

"Yes. He mentioned it."

"It's a small world. I used to make all of her dresses when they lived in Ramat Gan. A lovely person. A lovely couple. I'm glad that he's the one who's going to hold the service."

Again Yitshaak shrugged. The laws of the country forbade secular funerals, and it was simply a matter of convenience to contact Levinsky, who happened to live in the neighborhood.

"He's a fine old man," Esther went on. "Everyone likes him; admires him, I should say. More—depends on him. He was in Auschwitz, did you know that?"

"Yes. He mentioned that too."

"That wasn't easy for a rabbi. And not only because of the Germans, mind you. Because of our own. You can imagine what sort of a rabbi he must be if he still managed to command people's respect in a place where it was impossible to evade answering certain questions that would be asked."

"I understand."

"Do you?"

Yitshaak gazed about the room. On the coffee table, with its lace doily spread under glass, was a folded newspaper that he had bought on his way to the hospital in the morning. He took it up and began scanning the pages. His eyes burned with sweat, and after a short time, even without looking up, he became aware that Esther was watching him expectantly. Rooted to the same spot in the center of the room, her transparent, inverted image—the white blur of her face and her folded arms—stared up at him from the depths of the glass. He found it impossible to speak. It was the mention of Levinsky again, the possibility that remained of hope and peace, the chance that if he spoke to the bearded old man just once more, one of his phrases, perhaps one final word that he loosed upon the desolation, would come back to roost with an olive branch. He raised the paper, frowning, and tried to resume his reading. There was an article about the necessity of conserving water during the khamsin, the heat wave, and another, a letter to the editor from an engineer living in Jerusalem, about the dangers of exhaust fumes from cars polluting the air.

". . . greater volumes of oxides," he read, the words blurring before his eyes. This time he looked up. Quite suddenly, the light in the room seemed to have diminished. Outside, above the red roof of the schoolhouse, the pale-blue sky was becoming translucent.

"What time is it?" he asked.

"I don't know. It's getting late. I ought to go. I'll tell Zvi to drive straight to the hospital tomorrow morning. There's no sense in his coming here first."

"I'm not going," Yitshaak said.

"Where?"

"To Petach Tikva. To the funeral tomorrow. You and Nira will have to go alone."

"I don't understand."

"I'm staying at home."

"Aber ich kann nicht verstehen," she repeated, lapsing from Hebrew into German in her astonishment. "Why?"

"It was something you said."

"When?"

"When I came back from the hospital."

"I didn't say anything. What did I say?" Her eyes, clouded, suddenly cleared and widened in remembrance. With her left arm raised, unconsciously repeating the gesture she had made in the doorway, she repeated the words in a bewildered voice; the Hebrew phrase that had involuntarily escaped from her when she first heard of her nephew's death—the traditional invocation upon hearing evil news:

> "Blessed art Thou O Lord our God who art the
> true judge in Israel."

"It seemed to me—unfair," said Yitshaak. "An eight-year-old boy. I told Levinsky, but he said they were part of the ritual too. I'd forgotten. I haven't been to a funeral since Papa died. Levinsky said that the same words would be repeated tomorrow, over the grave. I told him that if that was the case, I wouldn't go."

"But why? Why?"

"Don't you understand? 'A true judge . . .' How can I have any part of that? That boy was—"

"What?"

Yitshaak shook his head.

"What was he? What?" Esther repeated, leaning forward, touching the edge of the coffee table with her knees. A drop of sweat trembled from the tip of her nose. From outside, through the open door, he heard the rumble of a truck on the road, and the faint, high drone of an airplane, coming in, or going out, over the sea.

"What? Tell me," she said, but Yitshaak remained silent. "Innocent," was what he had begun to say. In some way, he wanted to protest that his eight-year-old son, who had been condemned to suffer so and to die from cancer of the lymph nodes, had been innocent. He said nothing because while the explanation was forming on his lips, it had occurred to him for the first time that, if anything, her own faith, like Levinsky's, had taken the condemnation of innocence into account. Esther's faith had survived three and a half years in Belsen, where her husband, a rich furrier from Berlin, had died of typhus, and from which her daughter, a girl of thirteen, had been deported to Auschwitz in a sealed boxcar and gassed.

"No," said Esther. "It's not easy. Never think, not for one moment, that one simply accepts it all once and for all, and that's all there is to it."

"Then what? Tell me."

"Ah—" She smiled, blinking her eyes rapidly in the gathering darkness. The drop of sweat still trembled from the tip of her nose.

"Von Tag zu Tag."

He stared at her without understanding.

"Taeglich—daily," she repeated. "Und jeden Tag. One must struggle every day."

He pressed the heels of his palms into his eyes. No, there was something more. It wasn't simply a matter of acceptance. He knew, in time, he would come to accept the death, and even the suffering, of his son. That was natural, almost instinctive, a process of the mind protecting itself. Even now, amidst the wheeling, fading lights in the darkness behind his tightly shut lids, he found it hard to summon up the boy's features. It required all his effort to recall the pinched face he had seen that morning, when the doctor had lifted up the sheet on the hospital bed. The snub nose and the wide mouth, like Nira's. The tiny mole—where was it exactly? On the left cheek, beneath the eye. . . . No. It wasn't acceptance that he rebelled against. It was something else—something which seemed to him to be monstrously humiliating. Every day, the woman before him was struggling not so much to accept the suffering inflicted upon the innocents in the camp, but to—what? Yitshaak looked at her: the drop of sweat had gone from her nose. Yes, he thought, to sanctify it. She blessed God, her tormentor, and that same degradation would be required of him if he attended the funeral tomorrow. But to what end? Why? What purpose would it serve? She raised her head, and met his glance with those imperturbable eyes. . . . Reconciliation. The promise of peace.

Yitshaak stood up; the springs of the sofa creaked.

"When will you tell Nira?"

"I . . . Now," he said.

"Yitshaak?" his wife called out in a voice that was muffled by the pillow. "Who is it? Yitshaak? Is that you?"

The room was half dark. One ray of sunlight, streaming between two slats in the shutters, lit up the corner of the wall opposite the bed.

"Did I wake you?" he asked.

"No, no; what time is it?"

"Almost six."

"That late? My God. Have you had your dinner?"

"I had a late lunch," he said. "I'm not hungry."

"You mustn't be ashamed to ask Esther to make you something."

"I will, when I get hungry," he said, coming forward and sitting down as gently as he could on the edge of the bed. His wife smiled with her wide mouth, and turned her face toward the corner where the light was now red. One strand of hair, dark and stringy with sweat, lay on her cheek. She breathed deeply. Maybe she wanted to sleep some more. Yitshaak made a motion to rise.

"No, don't," she told him. Her left hand rose and fell. "Stay a little while."

"Esther wants to know if you remember Lani Goldman's address."

"Natanya. Number twelve Weizman Street."

"I thought she went away on vacation."

"She did. I forgot. They went to Naharia. I think they're staying at the Dolphin House."

"I'll tell Esther."

"Are you going to phone Lani?"

"I thought I'd send a telegram."

"Would you do me a favor?"

"What?"

"Call her, would you? Speak to her yourself. I'd like her to be with us tomorrow if she could."

"Nira?"

"What, dear?"

He reached out for her left hand, but simultaneously she brushed the strand of hair away from her cheek. His hand fell on the bedcovers by her side.

"Where are you going?" she asked him.

"Can I get you something? A cup of tea?"

"No, no, that's all right. But you go ahead. Get yourself something to eat. You won't forget to call Lani?"

"If that's what you want."

"Yes, do," she said. "Please. Get her to come."

Esther was waiting for him, against the rail. Yitshaak stood near the wall while she finished reciting the evening prayer.

" '. . . and arranges in order the stars in their watches in the firmament according to His will. . . .' "

A breeze, imperceptible at the height of the balcony, stirred the dusty leaves of the eucalyptus trees, and their dry rustling, merging now and again with her murmuring voice, was the only sound to be heard.

" '. . . and the darkness . . .' "

The breeze died away. " '. . . for ever and ever. Blessed art Thou O Lord our God who brings on the evening twilight. Amen.' "

Yitshaak looked at the sky, which was paler than in the afternoon, and even more luminous. A mass of dark clouds blown in from the sea had settled above the southern horizon, and although the sun had been gone for some minutes, a fiery streak of light lingered over the waves.

"Was Nira awake?" Esther asked.

"She wants me to call Lani."

"Did you tell her you weren't going?"

"I will. Later."

"When?"

It got darker. Here and there a light shone in a window. The sky too, still blue, was softly lit as though from within. Black ragged clouds drifted east.

"When?"

The first star of the evening gleamed in the southern sky, directly above a telephone pole on the road. The drift of the clouds in the opposite direction made it appear to be racing west. Another one, much dimmer, more distant, infinitely farther away in space, appeared beneath the first, and that too, because of the drift of the clouds, seemed to be racing out to sea. Yitshaak clung with both hands to the railing while the stars reeled above his head, and yet remained where they were, bound together above the telephone pole and the road.

"Well?"

He heard a dog bark. The clatter of supper dishes drifted to him from open windows.

"Then don't tell her," Esther whispered. "Don't say anything."

"I must."

"Not if you go."

"I can't."

"Go."

"I can't," he said. "Don't you think I would if I could?"

He now faced her. She answered without looking at him.

"Yes."

More and more stars flickered through the thinning clouds.

"Yes," she said. "I know. The final humiliation. You think I don't remember? How many times at the camp didn't I think: Ah, curse Him. Curse Him. Curse Him and have done with it. Still . . ." She pressed her palms together. "Still, one must live."

He nodded, and to calm himself, tried to identify the few constellations that he knew: the Milky Way, the Big Dipper—in Hebrew, the Great Wagon—that was just visible in the north.

"What is it?" Esther asked him. "What's the matter?"

He was weeping. He pointed one finger at the sky. All the clouds had gone, and all motion had ceased. In its place, from horizon to horizon, countless stars were shining, arranged in a vast, quiescent and eternal order that Esther had blessed, and from which he felt excluded by the tumult in his heart.

THE GROOM
ON ZLOTA STREET

In the winter of 1906, when he was twelve years old, my father, his parents, and his cousin Yechiel lived in a little shop on Mila Street in Warsaw, where my grandfather made carriage whips. Yechiel peddled the whips to grooms and drivers all over the city.

Opposite the shop was the entrance to a Russian military barracks, a huge stone building with an iron gate, that was guarded by two armed sentries who marched up and down the length of the cobblestone street.

At dawn, every morning, the boy looked out the cellar window and told Yechiel when the soldiers were at opposite ends of the street, and it was safe for him to leave the shop.

"Now, David?"

"Not yet," said the boy, and Yechiel slipped the pack off his back and rubbed his narrow shoulders where the straps cut into them.

"Now?" he asked.

"They're together at the gate."

"No rush. No rush. Just tell me when," said Yechiel.

"Did they pull your beard yesterday?"

"Only a little."

"Why don't you shave it off?"

"The Law forbids it."

Yechiel fingered his wispy beard, which grew only on his chin. The boy said, "One of them is looking this way."

"It can't be helped," said Yechiel, "I must go." He slipped the pack on his back. The tips of the long whips touched the ceiling. He said, "God be praised. God provides. He has given me as a customer the groom on Zlota Street. We must thank Him for that."

Yechiel went up the creaking stairs. The boy pressed his cheek against the cold glass. Then he heard the front door open and close, and he looked out the window. He saw Yechiel, from below, in front of the shop. His scraggly beard blew in the wind. One of the soldiers looked at him. The long thin bayonet on his rifle glinted in the sun. Yechiel turned to the right, away from the soldier, and quickly passed the cobbler's shop. The soldier stopped.

David stumbled up the stairs into the kitchen, where his father said, "You can't help Yechiel."

"Mama!" the boy cried out. "Make Papa let me go!"

His mother said, "Hush!" and peered out the window.

"Mama? What's happening? Is that soldier pulling Yechiel's beard?"

"Only a little," she said.

They worked in the other room. The boy scraped and shaved birch rods, around which his father wrapped strips of wet leather. He stitched them up, and sewed on the long, tubular lashes. Then he stitched a red tassel to each tip. There was no stove in the room. In the morning, they moved their bench to be warmed by the sunlight that streamed through the single oval window over the door. In the afternoon, it grew so cold that they could see their own breath. The boy suffered from chilblains. His fingers were red and puffy. It hurt to handle the knife; he often cut himself. His father worked opposite him, holding the rod between his knees and one end of the lash taut between his strong white teeth. He was a handsome man with wide dark eyes and a curly black beard.

He said, "Papa, I've been thinking. Maybe Yechiel should talk with the rabbi."

"What for?"

"Maybe the rabbi would give him permission to shave off his beard."

"The Law forbids us."

The boy sensed his father was ashamed because he'd given in to Mama's fears and sworn on his life never to accompany Yechiel in the morning.

"You can't protect him," she had cried. "They'll murder you both."

She often wept, and her lips twitched. The boy knew she blamed herself for everything because she had invited Yechiel to live with them after his mother—Mama's sister Sarah—had died. Yechiel hardly made a living; he suffered for nothing.

That night, after supper, Yechiel wiped his greasy fingers on his beard and said, "There's a new stable on Iron Street. I was there over an hour today talking to the groom."

"Is that so?" said the boy. "Did he buy any whips?"

"He told me to come back and see him next week."

"Who bought one today?"

"Nobody," said Yechiel. "But, God willing, I'm sure to sell some tomorrow."

"Really? How many will he buy?"

"Who?"

"Why, the groom on Zlota Street," said the boy.

"Who told you about him?"

"You did. Don't you remember? This morning."

"Did I?" said Yechiel. "Ah, if I want, the groom on Zlota Street would buy them all."

The boy said, "God be praised!"

He tossed and turned all night on the bed he shared with Yechiel in the workroom. Tomorrow was Friday, Sabbath eve, when Yechiel came home early to go to the mikveh on Marshalkovska Street for his ritual bath. The boy prayed, "Dear God, my Father in Heaven: obeying Thy Holy Law, my cousin Yechiel refuses to shave off his beard. Reward him for his suffering at the hands of the Gentiles. Make the groom on Zlota Street buy all of his whips!"

Such a sale would bring at least six rubles. What a Sabbath meal six rubles could buy: a carp, or chopped herring, potato pancakes, a roast chicken, and a bottle of wine. "Why, there'll be enough money for Mama to buy flour, raisins, and almonds. She'll bake a cake!"

The boy sat up and rubbed his eyes. His father said, "Good morning."

"Where's Yechiel?"

"He left early. Don't be alarmed! The soldiers left him alone today. It's snowing."

The boy ran to the window. The two soldiers, with their fur hats pulled down over their ears, stood by a smoky fire in front of the gate.

All morning, he pictured a roast chicken, between two flickering candles, on the Sabbath table. His mouth watered. "Heavenly Father, make the groom on Zlota Street buy all of Yechiel's whips!"

The boy helped his mother, who was on her hands and knees, scrub the kitchen floor. She said, "Take off your dirty shoes and move the table out of the way."

The Sabbath was coming! It seemed appropriate to him to walk with bare feet on the wooden floor, as though it were holy ground. He pushed the table into the corner, fed the fire, and washed and dried the plates till they shone and reflected his face.

His parents were out shopping when Yechiel came home, covered with snow. He put a few coins on the table, and said, "I sold two whips today—both on Kruvelska Street—for thirty kopeks apiece."

"Why didn't you go to the groom on Zlota Street?" the boy asked. "I prayed that he would buy all your whips."

"So he would."

"Then why didn't you go to him? I don't understand. I asked God to reward you for your suffering. Don't you want Him to answer my prayer? Oh, I understand! You know He won't."

Yechiel said, "Come with me and see what God provides," and he handed the boy his coat and woolen gloves. They went out together into the cold. The boy slipped on a patch of ice in front of the tailor shop. Yechiel caught him under one arm, and shouted, "Don't stop." One of the soldiers by the fire shouted at them, but his words swirled away with the wind that drove the falling snow down the street. On the deserted Prospect, Yechiel walked west. He held the boy by the hand. Thick, wet snowflakes stuck to his eyelashes; the wind howled.

They crossed the Prospect and headed east along a narrow street, between red-brick buildings with shuttered windows. They passed the mounted statue of a man holding up two crossed swords. The boy thought he heard church bells ringing. He saw a woman smoking a cigarette in a doorway.

At last, Yechiel led the boy through a gate and into the courtyard of a five-story house. He wiped the snow from his eyes and made out an iron stairway, hung with icicles, and to the right, a double wooden door.

"Your honor!" cried Yechiel in Polish, but using the Russian form of address. "Your honor, open the door!"

"Who's there?" a muffled voice replied.

"The Jew," said Yechiel, and the door opened, throwing a ray of light on the falling snow. The man inside, wearing a leather apron, said, "The Jew! What do you know? The Jew has changed his mind! Welcome! Who's that with you, Jew?"

"Only my young cousin," said Yechiel. "Won't your honor let us in?"

"Come in, by all means," said the man.

"Thank his honor for his kindness," said Yechiel.

"I thank your honor," said the boy. He thought that the young, clean-shaven groom, who had a cleft in his chin, was very handsome. He looked at Yechiel with his blue eyes, and said, "I knew you'd be back! You don't get an offer like mine every day."

"It's true," said Yechiel. "Your honor is very kind."

"Then you agree? How many is it to be? How many whips have you got in your pack?"

"Ten."

"Well, then, my usual offer stands. I'll buy the lot at a ruble apiece," said the groom.

"That's ten rubles!" said the boy. "What a deal!"

The groom laughed. "The little Jew knows a good deal when he hears one." He laughed again. In the stall behind him, a white horse stomped its hoofs on the wooden floor. The groom addressed Yechiel: "Well, what do you say?"

Yechiel fingered his beard. "Your honor is very kind."

"I thank your honor," said the boy. The groom laughed a third time. The horse again stomped its hoofs. Yechiel looked at the boy, and said, "His honor offers to buy ten whips at a ruble apiece in exchange for pulling my beard ten times. I have a choice! Praise God! There's always a choice to be made!"

"Yes or no?" asked the groom.

"No," said Yechiel. "I thank your honor, but not today."

"No, eh?" The groom grabbed Yechiel's beard with one hand, and punched him in the face twice with the other. "Now, get out!"

Yechiel and the boy sat for awhile on the iron steps in the courtyard. The snow had stopped; a cloudy sky was almost dark. Yechiel spat blood. His left eye was swollen shut. He held the boy's gloved hands between his own, and said, "You always have a choice! Remember that and rejoice! Rejoice! Praise Him! God provides!"

THE WELL

Sunday. It's ten-year-old Micah, Aviva's kid, waiting in front of the dining hall just before lunch, who brings us the news: one of the Bedouin camels from Ahmed's camp two kilometers south of the kibbutz has strayed into our date grove to give birth. "Come and thee! Come and thee!" he cries. Buck-toothed, and with ugly brick-red hair like his mother's, he speaks with a lisp, spraying a fine mist of spit into the air that gives me the fantastic notion that he has somehow boiled over from the heat. "Juth for a minute," he insists. Grossman the mechanic is with me, pale and drawn from his morning's work in the machine shop and his attack of *shil-shul,* the chronic dysentery, which has flared up in the last two days. "Pleath," the boy pleads, but bathed in sweat, and absent-mindedly chewing on the ragged end of his drooping mustache, Grossman refuses with a shake of his head, and goes inside, slamming the screen door behind him and stirring up the flies. The boy takes hold of my hand.

"It'll only take a minute."

"Where's your mother?"

A hubbub around us, as more and more of the *chaverim*—the comrades, members of the collective settlement—arrive at the dining hall from the workshops and the fields. They are in much the same state as Grossman and myself, and do not care who knows it: sullen, completely exhausted by the heat, and oppressed by the prospect of a meager meal and an afternoon's work still to be done.

"Oh pleath, pleath," the boy begs, with the rising inflection, the sad whine of the ugly child who has already learned that he cannot command attention any other way. "You don't underthtand."

"Maybe after lunch."

"But that'll be too late. He'th going to kill it."

"Kill what? Who?"

"Oh, hurry!"

It's too much of an effort for me to argue or try and understand, and he knows it. Hand in mine, he leads me away, past the deserted machine shop and the cowshed where, attracted by the feed, hundreds of twittering sparrows are perched on the corrugated tin roof—the only life, it seems, besides ourselves, abroad on the desert at this hour of the day.

Just noon. At the date grove, row on row of the broad dusty leaves cast no shadow, offer no refuge from the sun.

"Look!" says the boy.

"Where?"

I shield my eyes with my hand, and there, in the direction that he points, just beyond the line of trees to the south, is a camel with her colt that couldn't have been born more than an hour before. Beside them, on the ground and swarming with flies, is the bloody sack. The colt, waist high, as yet with only a rudimentary hump, all knees and huge splayed toes, jerks its head convulsively as it sucks at the pendulous swollen udders of the mare.

"Promith me!"

"What?"

"You won't let him kill it, will you?"

"Who, Micah, what are you talking about?"

This time, he only has to turn his head. To my left, ten feet away, and apparently watching us all the while, is a young Bedouin with a rifle, squatting on his hams against one of the trees.

"Shalom."

"And peace; peace unto you," he replies, speaking Hebrew with a thick Arabic accent. Under the kaffiah that shadows his eyes is a rather handsome, intelligent face; high cheekbones, a hooked nose, and a thick black mustache that droops down to the corners of his mouth.

"Athk him yourthelf. He thayth he'th going to kill it. Why?" says the boy, and the Bedouin, for an answer, glances up to indicate— what? In the torpor engendered by the heat, it takes me a moment to fully understand. I too, as though compelled, look up at the cloudless sky from which the sun has bleached all the color, leaving a white, translucent haze that dazzles the eyes.

"Tell me why!"

It's the drought, of course. I try and explain to the boy. Now, in the middle of November, what little autumnal rains the Bedouin depend on to water their herds is more than six weeks overdue.

"But what about their well?"

"Ah, now that's just the trouble. Their well has all gone dry. The colt has to be killed so that their children will have the milk to drink. You wouldn't want the children to die of thirst, would you?"

"I don't care."

"Micah!"

"Ith our well dry too?"

"Not yet; no."

"Why not?"

"It's deeper."

While we have been talking, the Bedouin has opened the bolt of his rifle—an old Lee Enfield .303—and inserted a cartridge with a click that rivets our attention to the oiled barrel gleaming in the sun. When he stands up in his soiled, billowing pantaloons, the boy cannot suppress a shout that makes the mare swivel her head in our direction. She apparently has just become aware of us, and, with a kind of comical, bewildered ferocity, lets hang her protruding underlip, and bares her teeth. The startled colt has stopped sucking, and skitters backward, with its shaky forelegs locked together, and the back spread awkwardly apart. For the first time, I catch a glimpse of its bitten cord, already withering from its belly like a dead vine.

"Chaver! . . . But comrade!" the boy shouts.

"Micah, come here. Come away."

"Comrade, don't!"

"Come away, I tell you. It's none of our business."

"You promithed!"

"No. There's nothing I can do."

I catch him by the hand and drag him away. At the cowshed, the echoing crack of the shot rouses the sparrows, who rise in a dark, twittering mass, circle the silo twice, and begin once again to settle on the sloping tin roof.

Grossman is still in the dining hall when I get back, sitting alone at a corner table.

"Where's the kid?" he asks.

"I left him at the nursery."

"Aviva was looking for him."

"I know. I saw her. How's the stomach?"

"O.K."

"Really better?"

Obviously forcing himself to keep up his strength, he is eating a plate of white goat's cheese and chopped cucumbers, washing down mouthfuls of the stuff with sips from a cup of cold water.

"The water'll give you cramps."

"No," he says, "I really feel better. So the Bedouin are beginning to slaughter their herds."

"You heard the shot. The kid was terribly upset."

"It's a shame."

"I read in yesterday's paper that the government says if the drought keeps up, they'll try and relocate the tribes to better grazing land up north."

"The government." He grimaces. With a sour expression on his face, wiping off his mustache, he pushes away the plate of food. "Who is doing the shooting?"

"One of the younger men. Good-looking. He speaks a little Hebrew, I think."

"Don't tell me. Not Ali?"

"Which one is Ali? . . . Oh." I remember Ali, Sheik Ahmed's oldest son, with whom Grossman had struck up a friendship two years before, when, for a season, both of them were shepherds, pasturing their herds together some thirty kilometers or so north of here.

He goes on, "It's a damn shame. By the time the government decides to do anything for them, it'll be too late."

"Not necessarily."

"You know it as well as I do. What's the use? By the time it goes through all the official channels to provide relief, they'll have slaughtered all their young animals. What'll they do come spring?"

"They'll manage."

"They'll starve. That's what."

Then he is silent. All around us, like insects in amber, each sound

in the room seems embedded and preserved in the thick air,
yellowed by the sunlight streaming through the windows: the
clatter of tin forks, the scrape of plates, the murmur of the comrades' voices, and, pervading all else, the buzz of the flies that are
so fat and lazy when they alight you can squash them with a
finger.

"Ali, eh?" he asks. "I haven't seen him in over a year. What do
you think? Maybe I ought to go over and have a talk with him."

"What you ought to do is go back to your room and lie down."

He gives me an ironic glance and is partly right. It's not his
health alone that concerns me, but a reluctance, as elected secretary, more or less a kind of first among equals, general manager
of the settlement, to allow the kibbutz to become officially in-
volved in Bedouin affairs at all.

"No," I tell him.

"Why not? We were friends."

"You asked my advice and I'm telling you. If they really would
like us to help them, let them take the initiative for once—just for
once—and come to us."

"I can't see any harm in just talking to Ali."

But there is. That's the trouble, and Grossman knows it as well
as I, in spite of any personal relationship he may have cultivated
with the Sheik's son. For eleven years now, since the establishment of our settlement in the desert by force of arms, we have
lived in a state of truce with Ahmed's tribe, no more and no less.
Time and time again, experience has taught us that when we so
much as offer them any material assistance, much less demon-
strate a willingness for a real peace, it is refused, and taken for
nothing but a display of weakness on our part, a loss of face as far
as they are concerned.

"No," I continue, "I—" But Grossman interrupts by standing up.

"No matter. It was just a thought."

He leaves, but all afternoon in the secretary's office—a desk, two
rattan chairs and a metal filing cabinet—I can think of nothing else
while I should be at work checking a list of supplies to be bought
tomorrow in Beersheva.

". . . 12 kilos baking soda, 10 salt . . ."

Impossible to keep my mind on it. The office, adjacent to the
radio shack, stands on a little rise behind the dining hall, com-

manding a view of the desert to the south. Broken up by a network of wadies running east to west—dry water courses eroded by flash floods—the landscape always gives me the impression that it has been raked by the talons of some gigantic beast. Here and there, glaring in the sun, are white outcroppings of rock—ribs and spines and shoulder blades, with no effort of the imagination at all, only partly buried by the cracked earth. Yes. It is exactly as though some unimaginable animal has dug at the earth to bury the bones of its prey.

". . . salt, 15 kilos sugar, tea . . ."

Again and again my gaze returns to the window, but at this distance the black wool tents of the Bedouin encampment are indistinguishable among the chaotic pattern of the shadow cast by the afternoon sun on the broken ground. Once, and only for a moment, one of their camels is to be seen, silhouetted against the sky, and again—or is it my imagination?—I can hear the faint echo of a rifle shot borne on the rising wind. Four-thirty. Finished by now with his work at the machine shop, Grossman is there, I am sure of it, but to speak with Ali means nothing. That's the whole point. It is Ahmed himself who has always been responsible for most of the difficulties that exist between us. The absolute ruler of the tribe for over twenty years, he is terrified—and with some justification—that even the minimal communication between the two communities will undermine his feudal authority. I have seen him only once or twice, at the Kassit, or Morris'—cafés in Beer-sheva: a great hulk of a man, not without dignity, who wears a pointed little beard, and whose dark, unhealthy-looking skin reminds me, for some reason, of the color of a slice of apple left exposed to the air. Purportedly he is still possessed of a harem of twenty women or more, and his licentiousness is legendary. One story has it that one day, long ago, at the height of his powers, he came upon a beautiful fourteen-year-old Bedouin girl drawing water from a desert well, and unable to resist making overtures—pleading, threatening, promising her anything to get her to join his harem—he reduced the child to tears.

"Let me go," she begged. "If you don't let me go, I'll tell my father."

"And just who is that?" Ahmed wanted to know.

"A sheik. A very powerful sheik who'll cut off your balls."

"Who?" he laughed. "Which sheik?"

"Sheik Ahmed," was the reply.

Five-fifteen. Grossman shows up at the office, looking even worse than before, completely drained, with livid lips and feverish eyes.

"So you went."

"Yes." We walk back to his room and he talks. "Things are terrible there, worse than I imagined. Their well has been dry since the day before yesterday. What water they have will only last them to the end of the week, if they're lucky. They've made up their minds to slaughter most of their herds by then, sell the meat for what they can get in Beersheva, and maybe buy enough water to last them until the rains come."

"Did you speak to Ali?"

"I was right. It was he that you saw. He agrees with me absolutely. If and when the government acts to help them, it'll be too late."

The evening breeze has already begun blowing from the southwest, drying the sweat from our bodies with a chill, and whipping the sand across the ground with a rasping noise that sets the teeth on edge. We pause in front of the row of attached wooden shacks that serve as the bachelor quarters of the settlement.

"So Ali really was willing to speak with you."

"Of course. One must be willing simply to—make the effort."

"And Ahmed?"

Grossman laughs. "The old dog. Would you believe it? Ali told me he's developed a taste for European women in his old age. He's placed ads in English, French, and German newspapers for a new concubine—preferably young, fat and blond."

"But you didn't speak with him?"

"It wasn't necessary."

"He refused to see you?"

"Yes, but it doesn't make any difference. He'll soon be dead. Ali will be sheik. He has most of the authority right now. I tell you, this is something new. Times have changed."

"I see. And just what did Ali propose?"

"Nothing. He just told me what was happening. Of course, I could see it all with my own eyes. They're desperate. He . . . No. He didn't propose anything."

"But you did."

"No. . . . That is, I suggested . . . Actually, I wanted to speak with you first."

We go inside his room that resembles a cell with its iron cot and tiled floor. Grossman insists on making coffee, squatting on his hams in front of the kerosene burner in the same posture as Ali against the date palm. Interesting, the similarities between them. It is never so apparent to me as now. Both of them, Arab and Jew, born in the country, reared here, feeling completely a part of it, even resemble each other physically, affecting the same drooping mustache that is probably Turkish in origin, signifying virility. The water begins to boil on the blue flame.

"Yes," repeats Grossman. "You'll see for yourself. Times have changed."

Does he really believe it? I don't know. Maybe it's so. In any case, what I, as a European immigrant, can never fully comprehend, is the significance of that mustache or peculiar crouch; the sense of utterly belonging in this country of his birth. Whatever the truth concerning the Bedouins may be, it is that which is at the heart of Grossman's passionate desire to effect a rapprochement with the tribe. Knowing no other home, he appreciates and respects the Arab's sense of possession for a land that he loves as well. He speaks fluent Arabic. The fact that he fought against Ahmed, who attacked the settlement on the final night of its establishment, seems to him beside the point. Being young, it is the present that counts for him—this moment alone, and the future, when the development of the land that he loves will depend first and foremost on peace.

"Sugar?"

"No thanks."

He hands me a cup, and sits on the cot.

"You realize this is the chance we've been waiting for."

"Maybe."

"But I told you," he says, "Ali will soon be sheik. If we can just establish good relations with him now . . ."

"But it isn't as if we haven't tried before. What about the drought four years ago? It was the same thing. They refused any help, and then—when was it? You remember. That little girl with appendicitis." He remembers, nodding his head sadly in the diminishing light. Two summers ago, rather than trust us to take one of their children into Beersheva for an operation, they apparently preferred to see her die.

"Still, this is different," he insists. "Ali is different from the old man. He spent almost a year in Jaffa, did you know that? Working at the port. With Jews. That's where he learned to speak some Hebrew. For the first time, they're more than willing to accept our help."

"What exactly do you suggest?"

"What about our own well?"

"All right, so far as I understand."

"That's what I thought. We've probably more than enough water to see us all through."

"That I couldn't say."

"Well, enough for at least a week, if we're careful. The rains will be here by then."

"Then what you want is to have us share our water."

"Exactly."

"That's, of course, a decision that neither of us can make alone."

"I realize that," he tells me. "The whole kibbutz will have to decide. That's why I wanted to speak with you. We'll hold a meeting."

"When?"

"You should have seen the camp. They're rationing what water they have, and the kids have sores on their lips—the corners of their mouths. They surrounded me with tin cans, begging for water, as one would beg for alms."

He has neglected to light a lamp. In the gathering dark, his face is almost invisible, and his momentary anguish is communicated only by the timbre of his voice.

"When do you want me to call a meeting?"

"What? Right away. The sooner the better. Tonight, if you can. Right after supper."

"I'll see what I can do."

"Wonderful. Oh. I almost forgot. Tell the night watch to let Ali through, will you?"

"You asked him to come here tonight?"

Under his mustache, his teeth gleam faintly as he grimaces with a stomach pang or smiles to himself in the dark.

"Yes," he tells me. "Of course, about ten."

The meeting, held in the dining hall, attended by about sixty adult members of the settlement, is over by nine forty-five. Simple majority rules, and Grossman's motion is carried by almost two to one after Lev, the engineer who dug our artesian well four years ago, assures us that in all probability there will be enough water to supply the two communities for at least the next week if we are careful. It's agreed that the Bedouin are to be permitted to take as much as they need every morning without charge—on one condition imposed by Zvika, who holds forth from his bench for more than five minutes, his round face shining with sweat, and his eyes bloodshot from the cigarette smoke that hangs in the air. He is a tractor driver, a man of about twenty-eight, prematurely completely bald, and intensely self-conscious about it, so that even indoors his head is always covered by an army fatigue cap, with its peak turned up. A particularly doctrinaire and pedantic socialist, and an author to boot, he has recently published a book comparing the life of the modern kibbutz to the ancient Hebrew Essene and early Christian communes. His high-pitched voice drones on. Now, to illustrate some point he is making, he is actually quoting by heart from Philo, describing the life of the Essenic communes near the Dead Sea that were so much like our own.

" '. . . For none of them wishes to have any property of his own, but rather by joining together everything without exception, they all have a common profit from it. . . .' "

Grossman, glancing at his wristwatch, interrupts him impatiently.

"Philo! Who's Philo? What's this Philo got to do with it?"

"I'm discussing the principles upon which this kibbutz has been founded. Principles which . . ."

"But there's a motion on the floor. What's all this have to do with sharing the water with the Bedouin?"

"That's it. Aha! Exactly. Sharing. You are evidently proposing an equitable distribution of the water. All well and good, and in accordance with our principles. But we are dealing here with a feudal lord—a sheik, don't forget that. What's there to guarantee that Ahmed will distribute our water fairly among his own people? How can we be absolutely sure, for example, that it's not his harem alone, or his relations—who knows?—who are going to benefit? Do I have to tell you . . ."

"I've already explained," says Grossman. "Ali . . ."

"What do I care about Ali? Ahmed, Ahmed is still sheik, and whether you remember it or not, it was Ahmed who . . ." His shrill voice breaks off, but the rest of the sentence hangs over us as tangibly as the blue smoke. It was Ahmed who ordered the surprise attack on the settlement eleven years ago, and who was responsible for the murder and mutilation of Zvika's first wife, a girl of seventeen. "As a matter of fact," he resumes . . .

"I guarantee it," says Grossman.

"How?"

"You have my word. I guarantee a fair distribution of the water. I'll supervise myself."

Zvika shrugs. Aviva rises, yawning behind her hand, and suggests that such a guarantee be amended to the original motion. She is exhausted from working all day in the communal laundry, and wants to go to bed.

"Well?"

A show of hands, throwing a forest of shadows resembling pruned trees against the wall. The amended motion is carried unanimously, and we adjourn.

"Congratulations," I tell Grossman.

"Thanks. Yes. It's a beginning, at least. A step in the right direction."

Outside, the wind is blowing from a blue-black sky that is ablaze with the innumerable stars of the desert night. Grossman shivers as we walk back to his room. The cold is intense. It is as if the sun today had burned away the atmosphere of the earth, exposing us to a chill from outer space itself.

"Ali ought to be here by now. Would you like to come in for a cup of coffee?"

"No thanks. I'm tired. Bed for me."

A little later, while brushing my teeth at the pump that stands outside the row of shacks, I catch a glimpse of them both through the window of Grossman's room. They are standing in the corner, by the orange crate that serves as a bookcase, talking together with cups of coffee in their hands. Once again, their physical resemblance is striking. They are even the same height, and but for the slightly darker cast of the Bedouin's skin, might be taken for blood relatives, cousins, or even brothers, perhaps, with their high cheekbones and long mustaches that emphasize their thin lips. Are they speaking Arabic or Hebrew? I am too far away to tell. The Bedouin suddenly laughs, touching Grossman on the upper arm. It is not hard to imagine that they are recalling the memories they have of shepherding together, near Halutza. Now Grossman is laughing too, holding his nose. I was right. They are talking about shepherding—the stench of the long-haired sheep, the lonely hours spent under the shade of the cypress tree, with the shared, stale loaf of bread on the grass between them, and the goatskin water bag passed from hand to hand.

Monday, just after dawn, it begins. For almost four hours now, patiently queued in the blazing sun, a long line of Bedouin women —perhaps a hundred of them or more—dressed entirely in flowing robes of black wool, with only their eyes showing, and strings of Turkish coins sewn onto their veils, draw water from the spigot outside of the cowshed. There is no sound but the twittering of the sparrows and the tinkle of coins as, one by one, they bend down and fill the tin cans they have brought with them. Occasionally, on their arms, a naked infant, covered with flies, is to be seen, but it too, as though enjoined by some mysterious command, makes no noise, but only gazes about with solemn, feverish eyes. Grossman and I are supervising. Just from the look of him, he feels no better, worse perhaps, than last night. The exhilaration of getting his motion passed and making arrangements with Ali has worn off. Periodically, he must excuse himself to go to the latrine, and when he returns with an embarrassed smile on his ravaged face, I plead with him to go back to his room and lie down.

"No, no, it's all right. I promised."

He dozes a little, stretched out in the shadow cast by the overhanging roof, while the black-robed women shuffle by. In the shed, a cow lows. I, too, begin to fall asleep, only to be abruptly awakened by a confused babble of voices, and a piercing shriek.

"What is it? What's happened?" Grossman rubs his eyes.

At the spigot, two of the women have gotten into a row. For some reason, one of them, holding up the line, evidently cannot make up her mind to fill up her rusty can or not. With her hands at her sides, clenching and unclenching one fist, she stares at the stream of water that splashes over the hem of her robe and bare feet, while now four or five of the others flap their arms and rage about her. Then, with another shriek, she is shoved aside, stumbling against Grossman who has come up to them, shouting in Arabic at the top of his voice. Silence again, sudden and complete, broken only by the wail of an infant from somewhere in the crowd.

"What's the trouble?" I ask.

"Turn off the water. . . . Just a minute," he tells me, and then, in Arabic, speaks to the woman who has been thrown against him. In a huddle on the ground, apparently mortified by her physical contact with a strange man, she buries her veiled face in her hands and emits nothing but a high-pitched, quavering wail. It is more than a minute before he can get her to answer. Then, listening attentively, with a puzzled expression on his face, he turns to me.

"I don't understand."

"What does she say?"

"It just doesn't make sense. She says that she and her husband are very poor. They will starve because they own only two milch goats that will die of thirst unless they can get water."

"Then why doesn't she take it?"

"That's what's so confusing. She says she can't afford it."

"Are you sure?"

"Positive."

"But tell her it's free. She can take as much as she needs without charge. Didn't you explain that to Ali?"

"Of course."

"Well, didn't he tell them?"

Again, Grossman questions her, but this time she refuses to answer altogether. It is impossible to determine her age, or even the shape of her body underneath that robe. Only her eyes are visible.

"Useless." Grossman straightens up. The other women have fallen back in a silent semicircle around us. "I just don't get it. There's obviously been a misunderstanding of some kind."

"What are you going to do?"

"I don't know. Ask Ali, I guess."

"Now?"

"I suppose so."

"Wait here, I'll bring the Jeep and go with you."

"No, no, there's no need."

"Do as I say. You're in no condition to drive."

With one hand to his head, he closes his eyes and makes a gesture as if to shake off the weakness that has hold of him.

"I don't know," he says. "Maybe we ought to wait."

"For what?"

"They really can't afford it."

"Afford what? What are you talking about?"

"If we drive over to the camp now, we'll be considered guests. You know their laws of hospitality. They'll feel obliged to slaughter a sheep for a meal."

"You wait here."

The communal Jeep is kept in the machine shop, but it takes me over twenty minutes to locate Chaim, who has charge of the keys. He is working in the shack that houses our electric generator, repairing a worn fan belt. I could have spared myself the effort. By the time I drive back to the cowshed, Ali is there. He has apparently just ridden over from the encampment on a small white mare that one of the women holds by the bridle as he dismounts and shakes hands with Grossman, who begins talking to him at once, in a low, anxious voice. They are speaking in Hebrew as I come up, each with his forehead almost touching that of the other, and their hands clasped behind them.

"Then you did tell them," Grossman is saying. The Bedouin nods.

"But I still don't understand. If they know we are not charging them anything, why does the woman say she can't afford it?"

"It's nothing."

"There must be a reason."

"She's talking about the tax."

"What tax?"

"A half a pound."

"For what? Whose?"

"My father's. For the use of the water."

Ali is smiling. He is having difficulty in speaking Hebrew so quickly. Now, very slowly, searching for each word: "You mustn't bother yourself."

"Do you mean to tell me that your father is taxing them a half a pound per person for the use of water from our well?"

"But of course."

Grossman is silent. Behind us, an infant gives a stifled cry, and the mare tosses her head and chomps at her bit.

"Let me get this straight."

"But I have already explained," says Ali. "There's no need to concern yourself. This is—" He completes the sentence in Arabic: "—our affair entirely. Yes, that's it. It's the law. The tribe must always pay the sheik for the right to draw water from the well."

"But the water is ours."

The Bedouin gives a barely perceptible shrug.

"Don't you understand?" says Grossman. "It's impossible. I gave my word. The whole point is for us to share with all of your people fairly. An equal distribution."

Again, the Bedouin apparently cannot get the drift of the Hebrew. Grossman must translate.

"Equal?"

"Yes," says Grossman. "That woman, for example. What about those who can't afford it?"

"Equal?" the Bedouin repeats, and then, giving up, he lapses entirely into Arabic.

"What's he say?" I ask Grossman.

"He says it's the law. It's always been the law. He says it's the lord's—his father's—right as sheik to tax them, just as it was his father's before him, and before that, long before . . ."

"Before what?"

"He didn't say."

I glance at the Bedouin, who is looking beyond me, beyond the sloping tin roof of the cowshed and the date grove, toward the desert where the shadows are diminishing as the sun slowly ascends toward noon. . . . Before. Before us, is of course what he means; long before our possession of the land, our settlement and government, when free, or at least subject only to his own law, the Bedouin roamed the desert that belonged to him alone.

"No," says Grossman. "It's out of the question. At the meeting, I promised . . ." and then, in a final effort to make himself understood, he too continues in Arabic. Before he has finished, the sun has reached its zenith. His eyes are glazed, his face is streaked with sweat. The Bedouin says nothing until, with a hopeless gesture, one palm upraised, he abruptly turns on his naked heel and walks with dignity toward the waiting mare. The little horse takes a mincing step as Ali swings himself into the wooden saddle and shouts a word of command to the waiting women, one of whom catches his reins as he leads them away. For almost a minute after they are out of sight, their dust hangs in the air. Grossman coughs, and with averted eyes, and saying nothing, goes down on one knee to the spigot, where he catches a few drops of water that cling to the spout, and moistens his parched lips.

Tuesday and Wednesday. Not a cloud. No sign of rain. The colorless sky is empty but for the flocks of ravens that wheel in gigantic circles above the Bedouin camp. From morning to night they are to be seen like spots before the eyes, the symptom of some madness induced by the heat of the sun. Now there can be no doubt of it; without water, the Bedouin are slaughtering the remainder of their herds to be sold as meat in the market on Thursday in Beersheva. Although I am sure he is aware of what is happening, Grossman makes no mention of it. All day Tuesday he is too sick even to get out of bed. Some of the women take turns bringing him tea and toast, and emptying his bedpan, and for the rest of the time he lies perfectly still, with his face to the wall. Then, as is sometimes the case, on Thursday morning, although he is greatly weakened, his stomach spasms have subsided sufficiently for him to get up. Restless and inordinately thirsty, he haunts my office where I am busy writing a letter to Tnuva, the cooperative marketing organization of the kibbutzim that is negotiating with us for the export of our dates overseas. For what seems to be an hour, he sits by the window facing south, sucking on an orange and brushing away the flies that settle on his face and arms.

"What do you think?" he asks at last. "I suppose it's really Ahmed's fault."

I put down my pen. "I guess so."

"Still, it's a shame. There must be something that can be done."

Then, for a while longer, he is silent. Again a ray of sunlight, riddled with dust, illuminates his face. In the past few days he has lost weight and looks somehow five years younger and more vulnerable than he really is—twenty-six or -seven at the most. The drooping mustache seems more of an affectation than ever, a pretense of manhood pasted on by a kid.

"I don't suppose Ali was here while I was sick."

"No."

"No, I didn't think so. He'll never come back now. . . . Strange. How well it was going that night when he and I had coffee in my room. Ai, if you only knew how sick of it all I am!"

"Of what?"

"This—hatred. Did you know that eleven years ago, the night of the attack, I was the one who found Chava?"

"Chava?"

"You remember. Zvika's wife."

"Chava. Yes."

"She was sleeping in her tent when they came. They slashed her with their long knives. She was still alive when I found her. Sometimes, you know, I still—have dreams."

"But you don't hate them."

"The Bedouin? I did. Oh, how I did. It's just—bloodshed. It makes me sick. All these years. Endless."

More silence. He rises abruptly from his chair.

"Who can say? I wonder if it'll do any good now."

"What's that?" I ask.

"It couldn't do any harm."

"What?"

"It might still help. You never know."

"I see. You want to go to their camp and try to speak with Ali again."

"Yes."

Now it is my turn to say nothing. He shreds the pulp from the orange rind with his teeth.

"It'll be unofficial, of course. No one here will ever know, except you and me."

"Then why tell me?"

"Because I thought you understood. Don't you see? It's better than not doing anything—letting it go on and on. What is there to lose?"

"I don't know."

"Nothing, I tell you. Come with me," he says. "You'll see."

I screw on the top of the fountain pen. My sweating wrist has smudged the ink on the letter. It will have to be done over again. "If that's what you really want."

"Yes."

We take the Jeep. South of the settlement, there is only a narrow dirt track that eventually leads to the Egyptian border, just north of Nitzana. Surrounded by the white rocks, we are in the valley of the bones, but even here, in the mouths of the wadies, there is still some scrub vegetation left alive, a gray-green stubble encrusted by the white shells of countless snails. Not a tree is to be seen.

"How far now?"

"A half a kilometer. Less," Grossman shouts. Ahead of us, and to the left, where the track intersects with still another narrower path that leads between the rocks, he slows down.

"Their well."

It takes me a moment to be able to distinguish the ruin as a ring of man-raised stones, about knee high, and plastered together with sun-baked mud. He shrugs and drives on, now off the track itself, and up the floor of a huge wadi that runs parallel to the patch among the rocks. When he stops, only one black tent can be seen to our right. The rest are apparently hidden around the bend of the wadi walls that are over ten feet tall.

"Where is everybody?"

"Hiding," Grossman explains.

"Are they afraid?"

"It's just the way they are with strangers."

"Well, there's Ali, at any rate."

"Where?"

He is standing with another man in the shadow of a huge boulder about fifty yards away, near the half-skinned carcasses of four or five freshly slaughtered sheep that lie on the ground covered by a cloud of flies. The blood and flies, the cry of the ravens whose shadows flit across the ground—even the untended fire of dried camel dung smoking in front of the tent—give the impression that a catastrophe has hit the camp. The naked child completes the picture. A little boy, perhaps six years old, with a swollen belly and shaven skull, emerges from the tent at our approach with a tin can in his hands. BRANDIED APRICOTS, printed in English, coming from God knows where, part of the label is clearly visible as he thrusts it before us, begging for water without a sound.

"Give him your canteen," whispers Grossman, "and wait here."

He starts forward. The child, for some reason, refuses to drink from the canteen itself. I must pour the water into the rusty can, but there is too much of it, and it spills to the ground.

"Wait!" I cry, but it is too late. He has already turned and disappeared once more into the tent. Now Grossman is talking, rapidly, and in an undertone, to Ali, in Arabic, standing with the bloody carcass of the sheep on the ground between them. The second Bedouin has taken a little step to the left, and for the first time I can see him clearly. It's the old man himself, Ahmed, the Sheik, fatter and older than I remember him, with a fuller beard that has turned completely gray. Still, unmistakably, it is he: carrying himself erect, with his shoulders back, and one hand playing with the hilt of a silver dagger stuck in the yellow sash around his waist. Ali has begun to talk too, for the first time, in a loud, clear voice. The old man glances at him, and, either because the sun is in his eyes, or because something his son has said amuses him, he screws up his face and shows his teeth in a grimace that could be taken for a smile. Behind me, the child, or someone, stirs in the tent, and when again I look around what happens next happens so quickly that it is only later, in retrospect, that I can visualize it all as a piece. Ali is talking, gesturing with his hands, and suddenly, without warning, Grossman has lunged at him, slipping on the bloody ground, so that he is only able to give the Bedouin a glancing blow on the right cheek with his fist. They are down, the both of them, and for the moment, incredulous, neither I nor the old man can make a move. He is still grimacing, the smile frozen on his face, his fingers spread on the hilt of the knife. A moment more, and both of us still remain where we are. Grossman is the first to get to his feet, staring stupidly down at the Bedouin who holds his hand to his cheek and rocks his head slightly from side to side. When I come up, the old man retreats another step to the left.

"What's happened?" I ask.

No answer. "What is it?" Still no response. With his mouth open, and the same stupefied expression on his face, Grossman reaches out his hand with the evident intention of helping Ali to his feet. "Tell me," I repeat. The hand, smeared with sheep's blood, is still extended, but now the Bedouin drags himself back on his elbows and spits on the ground with disgust.

"He blames us for everything," says Grossman, getting behind the wheel of the Jeep. "The fact that they've lost their herds—this morning, a child died—everything. There was nothing I could say. He says his father is right. We've taken their land, and now deny them water."

He tries to turn on the ignition, but fumbles with the keys. His hand is trembling. I glance up. The two Bedouin are standing in front of the tent. Something apparently has struck them as funny. The old man, at least, is laughing deep in his throat, with his head thrown back and his hand still on the hilt of his dagger.

I ask Grossman, "Why did you hit him?"

"He called me a dog of a Jew."

THE LAW

That whole summer, I wondered what my uncle Willi was going to do about his son. Danny would be thirteen on July twelfth, and as early as February, Willi talked about having his Bar Mitzvah at their Temple in Queens; the whole works—a service in the morning and a party for the family and their friends in the afternoon at their home.

"Nothing ostentatious, you understand," he told me. "Drinks and hors d'oeuvres. You know: franks, little kosher pigs in blankets, or lox on pieces of toast."

I said that maybe that was enough. "Why the service? You don't want to make him go through all of that speechmaking."

"Ah, but he insists," said Willi.

"Does he?"

"So help me. He says he wouldn't think of having one without the other, and his doctor says it's all right. The doctor says if he really wants to speak, then by all means. Treat him normal."

"What doctor?"

"Rhinehart. Didn't I tell you? Rhinehart's been treating him since last fall."

"Who's Rhinehart?"

"I thought you knew. Didn't Helene tell you? Rhinehart's a speech therapist. One of the big men in New York. He's connected with the Medical Center. Just since September, and he's done wonders."

"I'm glad to hear it."

"Will you come to the service?" he asked.

"When will it be?"

"The weekend after the Fourth. That Saturday, in the morning. The Fourth is on a Monday. That Saturday, the ninth," he said.

"Sure."

"Ten o'clock in the morning. Don't you forget now. Mark it down," he said.

I never thought he'd go through with it. For as long as I could remember, his son had a terrible stammer. Just saying "hello" was an effort. He shut his eyes and took a deep breath. His chin jerked up and down and spit gathered in the corners of his mouth.

"H-h-h-hello, Joe," he'd greet me. "How-how-how are ya?"

Silent, he seemed another kid, one with dark eyes, beautiful eyes, with long curly lashes. He had delicate hands; his bitten nails were always in his mouth. To avoid speaking he had developed the facility of listening attentively, fixing those eyes on you, with a faint smile on his lips, nodding or shaking his head as the occasion demanded, so that he gave the impression of following whatever you said with a kind of ravenous intensity that made you self-conscious about being able to speak normally. An intelligent defense. He was really brilliant.

"An A average in school," Willi told me, throwing his arm about the boy's shoulders. "He loves history," he added, as a kind of concession to me, and paused to let me test the boy's knowledge. Helene, his mother, looked alarmed. I remained silent, and the boy looked at me with gratitude. At the time, I was teaching American history to the tenth grade in a private school on the Upper East Side. It was easy to imagine Danny's suffering in class when he was called upon by his teacher to recite, while the other kids laughed behind their hands or mimicked him.

That was in February. Came the spring and I didn't see much of them. I spent most of my time in the Forty-second Street Library doing research for my Ph.D. thesis on the Alien and Sedition Acts. A couple of times in May Willi called me on the phone to invite me out to dinner, but I was too busy. He was really the only family I had left, but we were never close. Willi, who was my mother's younger brother, had been born in Germany. My mother had written and tried to persuade him to leave the country in 1935, but he wanted to study law at Heidelberg. The Nazis deported him to Bergen Belsen, where he managed to survive the war, coming to this country in 1947, just before mother died. He wrote a book about his experiences—*Mein Erlebnis*—that was never published, but everyone who knew him felt they had read it anyhow, from the way he spoke of what had happened to him. He loved to talk, but if it was a blow to his pride that his son had so much trouble in getting a word out straight, he never let on.

"Stammering? What's a stammer?" I once heard him tell the boy. "It's a sign of greatness. . . . Yes, I mean it. Demosthenes stammered, and Moses. Moshe Ribenue. Moses our Teacher himself."

"M-M-Moses?"

"The luckiest thing that ever happened, believe you me."

"H-h-how l-lucky?"

"How many Commandments are there?"

His son held up ten fingers.

"Ten! There you are!" said his father. "Believe me, if he hadn't stammered he would have given us a hundred."

The boy laughed. His father had a way with words. He made a good living as a paper-box salesman for a company at New Hyde Park on the Island. I imagine he cleared over twenty thousand a year. He owned a red-brick, two-story, semi-detached house on Eighty-first Avenue in Queens, with a little rose garden in the back and a pine-paneled bar and rumpus room in the cellar where he intended to have the party after the Bar Mitzvah. I went out there for dinner the second week in May. We had a drink downstairs.

"You can't help it," he said. "I figure about thirty, thirty-five people. What can I do? Helene's family, friends from the office, the kid's friends from school, the rabbi and his wife. Thirty-five, maybe more. Helene says we'll have to serve them lunch. I thought maybe a cold buffet. We'll eat down here. I'm having it air-conditioned."

"It's a nice idea."

"It'll be a nice party, you wait and see. How about another Scotch?"

"Just a drop."

"Chivas Regal. Twenty years old. Like velvet water."

"Just a splash of water," I told him. "Where's Danny?"

"What's the time?"

"Just six."

"Be home any minute. He's at Hebrew school."

"How's he doing?"

"Wonderful. That rabbi does wonders. The boy can already read. Of course, it's all modern. To help him he has a recording of the Haftorah he has to say, put out by some company in New Jersey."

"Sounds like a wonderful idea."

"He's reciting from Numbers."

"I don't know too much about it."

"It's some of the Laws, and how the Children of Israel organize themselves in the march through the desert."

"And Danny likes it?" I asked.

"You should hear him. The rabbi, the doctor, Rhinehart—I told you: everybody helps. Ask him yourself."

He came home about six-thirty, with his notebook under his arm. He had grown a little since I saw him last, become a little leaner. His hands and feet were bigger. There was down on his cheeks and upper lip, but his speech was the same. He went through convulsions to say hello. When we sat down at the dinner table, he remained standing by his place, with a loaf of bread covered by a linen napkin set before him, and a black silk skullcap on the back of his head.

He mumbled, "B-b-b-b-aruch atar a-adonoi"—the Hebrew blessing of the bread—and when he finished, he wiped the spit from his lips with the back of his hand.

"How was that?" Willi asked me.

"Nice."

"Practice. Practice makes perfect."

His son lowered his eyes. Helene served the roast chicken and wild rice, with little brown potatoes.

"You never learned Hebrew?" Willi spoke to me again.

"No. I wasn't Bar Mitzvahed."

"Neither was I."

"Really?"

"In Germany, when I was growing up, it was—unfashionable to be given a Jewish education." He tore at a chicken wing with his teeth. "Once in a while in the camp I would run into somebody who could speak Hebrew. It's an ugly language, but it was nice to hear it spoken. It was verboten, of course, but still . . . How can I explain? It was something out of our past, the really distant past.

It somehow seemed to me to be the only part of our consciousness that was left—uncontaminated. Not like Yiddish. I always hated Yiddish. I used to pride myself on my command of German, the way I wrote particularly, a really educated style, but I learned to hate it. Sometimes for weeks I couldn't bring myself to say a word. The language of the SS . . ."

"T-t-t-tell about H-H-Heinz," interrupted his son.

"Eat your chicken," his mother said. The angry tone of her voice surprised me. She was a refugee from Germany who came here in 1936. I suddenly saw that she disapproved of Willi's imposition of the whole thing on the boy's consciousness. We finished the lemon meringue pie and coffee in silence; then Willi, the boy, and I went into the living room.

"Cigar?" Willi asked.

"No thanks."

He belched, lit up, and picked his front teeth with the folded cellophane. "How about a little brandy?"

"That'd be nice."

"Napoleon: the best," he said, pouring some into two snifters. "Wonderful. Too good. I'm getting too fat, I know. Soft," he said, patting his paunch. "The doctor tells me I ought to lose at least twenty pounds. An irony, eh? Did you know that when I got out of Belsen I weighed ninety pounds? Ninety, mind you, and now, like all Americans, I'm to die of overweight."

His eyes gleamed as though he derived satisfaction from the thought.

"A living skeleton," he went on. "You must have seen photos after the liberation of a place like that. I don't have to tell you."

He went on and on, while his son bit his fingernails.

"You can't know—thank God—not you, or Danny here, or Helene. No one who was not there can even guess what it was like to be so hungry, to be literally starving to death on two slices of bread a day, and a pint of watery soup with a snip of turnip in it, if you're lucky. Twice a week a spoonful of rancid butter, and an ounce of sausage or cheese. And the worst of it knowing that it's endless, knowing that no matter how hungry you are today there's absolutely no possibility of getting anything more to eat tomorrow but that the anguish will simply grow and grow and grow. . . .

Words. . . ." He shrugged. "What good are words to describe such things?"

He puffed on his cigar and said, "Everyone had two obsessions. Food first: dreaming about food, sitting down to a meal like we just had, and eating till you burst. And second: just staying alive so that you would be able to describe what was happening to you. Everyone wanted to write a book. Seriously. Just to tell the world, as though to convince ourselves as well that such things were really happening, that we were actually living through them. I wrote *Mein Erlebnis* in six weeks."

He waved the smoke away.

The boy leaned forward, with parted lips, drinking in his father's words. I suddenly understood Willi's compulsion to talk to the boy about the concentration camp. He was describing his greatest success: how he, among millions, had managed to survive.

Helene came into the living room with a bowl of fruit.

"An apple, Joe?"

"No thanks."

Willi peeled a banana, and changed the subject. He asked about my work.

"The Alien and Sedition Acts, eh?" he said. "Yes. . . . Yes, interesting and significant. . . . When was it again?"

"S-s-seventeen n-ninety-eight," said Danny.

"That's right," I told him.

Willi grinned. "I told you he loves his history."

"He's right a hundred percent."

"Who was it?" Willi went on. "President Adams, wasn't it? Against the Bill of Rights—the first suspension of habeas corpus."

"And M-M-Marshall," began the boy.

His father laughed with his mouth full of banana. "You can see for yourself he knows much more about it than me." The boy blushed. Willi said, "Still, I remember: No freedom of speech, hundreds of editors thrown into jail for criticizing the government, the prisons packed with dissenters."

"About twenty-five, all told," I said.

"You don't say. Just twenty-five?"

"That's it."

He grinned again. "How about that! America, you see?" he said to his wife. "Imagine. A whole stink over that."

"There was more to it than that," I told him.

"Of course, but still—a crisis! Genuine indignation over the fate of just twenty-five men."

"Yes, partly," I told him, suddenly weary from the dinner and the drinks.

"And the Jews?" he asked me.

"I don't understand."

"Did they persecute Jews?"

"The law was directed against foreigners, mostly—the British and the French. French spies, for example. There was a lot of spying going on, and the law forced a lot of foreigners to leave the country."

"But nothing was specifically directed against the Jews."

"No. Why should there have been?"

Willi laughed.

"What's so funny?" I asked him.

"Don't you know the joke?"

"Which one?"

"The SS man in Berlin grabs a Jew by the collar and kicks him in the shins. 'Tell me, Jew, who's responsible for all of Germany's troubles?' The Jew trembles. His teeth chatter. 'The Jews, of course,' he answers. 'Good,' says the SS man. 'The Jews and the bareback riders in the circus,' the Jew goes on. 'Why the bareback riders in the circus?' the SS man asks. 'Aha,' comes the answer. 'Exactly! So nu? Why the Jews?' "

The boy laughed until tears came into his eyes. It was as if he were delighted to find a release in a sound that he could express without impediment.

"Yes, yes," Willi continued, throwing the banana peel into an ashtray. "He laughs, but one must ask: Why the Jews? There's the psychology of a Heinz to contend with, and not an isolated pathological case either, but common. More common than you'd care to know."

"Have a piece of fruit," Helene told me.

"No thanks. Who's Heinz?" I asked.

"Herr Hauptsturmführer Berger," said Willi. "You know the type. Tall and blond, beautiful, really, the very image of manly perfection that you can see for yourself, today, in the movies. A movie star, so help me; six foot two at least, with straight blond hair, white teeth, dimples, blue eyes."

"But I still don't understand," I said. "Who is he?"

"*Was*," said Willi. "He *was* a guard in the camp. After the war the British caught him and he was tried and hanged. . . . *Was.* . . . Unfortunate. I mean it, too. Seriously. No one had the good sense to study him instead: how he used to stand, for example—very significant—with the thumb of one hand, his left hand, I remember, stuck in his belt, and the other grasping a braided riding whip that he would tap against his black boots. He was convicted of murder. One day he killed a child, a little girl of seven. . . . In the camp, some of the barracks had three tiers of wooden beds along the wall, bare planks to sleep on, 'boxen' in the jargon. We slept packed together. Often someone would die in the night, but it was impossible to move. We slept with the dead. . . . Where was I?"

"The child," I said.

"Ah, yes. One of the boxen in the women's barracks was coming apart; one leg was coming off. Three tiers, mind you; hundreds of pounds of timber. For some reason the child was on the floor, directly beneath it, on her hands and knees. Perhaps he—Heinz —had ordered it so. I don't know. I don't think so. She must just have been looking for something. A crust of bread, a crumb, perhaps, and in walks the Hauptsturmführer smiling all the while as though to charm the ladies, immediately sizing up the situation; perfect. The child beneath the rickety bed, the girl's mother, Frau Schwarz, in one corner, binding up her swollen legs with a few rags.

" 'Gnädige Frau . . . ,' he greets her—the mother, who stands up nervously twisting a rag about her wrist.

" 'Hilda!' she screams. Not even a Jewish name, mind you; a good German name. 'Hilda!' The child begins to rise, but it's too late. With a flick of his boot, a movement of that polished toe, our Heinz has already acted, kicking out the loose timber, bringing down the whole thing on the child's back. A broken back.

" 'Mama!' she cries. 'I can't move! My legs!' For a day and a half like that until she goes into convulsions and dies in her mother's arms. The woman comes to me and reproaches herself because she hasn't got the courage to commit suicide.

" 'After all,' she says, 'I have the means.' She's referring to the rags that she has woven into a noose. 'Just the courage is lacking. Mr. Levy, what's the matter with me?' She goes mad, and before she dies she wanders about the camp asking everyone to strangle her. She even comes to Heinz. It was just outside the latrines. I witnessed this myself. Apparently he doesn't even remember who she is. He shoos her away, those beautiful blue eyes clouded for just an instant in complete bewilderment.

" 'Verrückt,' he tells me. 'Insane.' With a shrug. I'm busy on my hands and knees scrubbing the concrete floor with a brush and a pail of lye and water, not daring to look up, blinded by those boots.

" 'Here, here, Levy. No, to the left. Put some elbow grease into it.'

"A fanatic for order and cleanliness, you understand. He used to speak with me a great deal. I couldn't imagine why. Perhaps because we were both about the same age. He would constantly ask me questions about the Jews—technical questions, so to speak, about our beliefs, about the Torah, for example, all the Laws. He seemed sincerely interested and, as far as I could tell, he was genuinely disappointed when he realized that I knew next to nothing and had been educated like himself as a good, middle-class German—*Gymnasium,* and two semesters åt Heidelberg. One day he was absolutely flabbergasted to find out that for the life of me I couldn't even recite the Ten Commandments. I couldn't get more than five, and not in order, either. 'Tsk, tsk, Levy.' He shook that beautiful head and began reciting them all.

" 'I am the Lord thy God who brought thee forth out of the land of Egypt, out of the house of bondage. . . . Thou shalt have no other gods before me.' Etc., etc. All of them, the whole business. Imagine the scene. It was a Sunday, I remember, rest day, the one day off from man-killing labor the whole week. I had gone outside the barracks to get a little sun. Imagine it, I tell you. A vast desert, our own Sinai surrounding us, rolling sand dunes, green wooden shacks set in rows. In the distance, the silver birch trees of the women's camp like a mirage. The wire mesh gate of the main entrance to my right that always reminded me of the entrance to a zoo. Here and there, scattered on the ground, all heaped together, the mounds of bodies, the living dead and the dead—stiff, open eyes, gaping mouths, all heaped together, indistinguishable.

It was early spring, and warm, with a weak sun, gray clouds, cumuli, with a flat base and rounded outlines, piled up like mountains in the western sky. I remember that distinctly—cumuli. It was a matter of life and death, learning to tell one type of cloud from another—the promise of a little rain. There was never enough water. Just two concrete basins to supply the entire camp. We were slowly dying of thirst in addition to everything else. I remember thinking that if the rain does come I shall try and remain outside the barracks as long as I can after roll call, with my mouth open. Crazy thoughts. What was it? Chickens, young Truthähne—turkeys drown that way in the rain, too stupid to close their mouths. Insane, disconnected thoughts while, according to regulation, I stood rigidly at attention, with my chin in, and chest out, my thumbs along the crease in my striped prison pants, as Heinz drones on and on.

" 'Honor thy father and thy mother. . . . Thou shalt not murder. . . .' On and on to the end, and then, with what I can only describe as a shy expression on his face, the explanation:

" 'We live in Saxony,' he tells me. 'Absolutely charming, Levy. Do you know East Prussia? Ah, the orchard and the flower beds —roses, red and white roses, growing in front of the church. My father's church. A pastor, Levy, and his father before him and before that. Three generations of pastors. When I was young, I thought I would go into the Church myself. I have the religious temperament.'

" 'Yes, sir. Jawohl, Herr Hauptsturmführer.'

" 'Does that astonish you?'

" 'Not at all, Mein Herr.'

" 'It does, of course. . . . Sundays. . . . Ah, a day like today. The church bells echoing in the valley and the peasants in their black suits and creaking shoes shuffling between those rose beds to listen to Papa thunder at them from the pulpit, slamming down his fist. "Love, my friends! It is written that we are to love our neighbors as ourselves." The fist again. "Love!" he shouts, and I would begin to tremble, literally begin to shake. Why, Levy? I often asked myself. You ought to know. Jews are great psychologists. Freud . . .'

" 'I don't know, Herr Hauptsturmführer.'

" 'A pity. . . . He preached love and all I could see from that front pew was that great fist—the blond hair on the backs of the fingers, the knuckles clenched, white. That huge fist protruding from the black cuff like the hand of God from a thunder cloud.' That was his image, I swear it. So help me, a literary mind. 'Die grosse Faust ist aus der schwarzen Manschette heraus gestreckt wie Gotteshand aus einer Sturmwolke. Yet, to be honest,' Heinz went on, 'he never struck me. Not once in my whole life, and I was never what you could call a good child, Levy. Secret vices, a rebellious spirit that had to be broken. And obedience was doubly difficult for the likes of me, but as I've said, whenever I misbehaved, he never once laid a hand on me. . . . Love. . . . He spoke about love and was silent. Talk about psychology! That silence for days on end; all he had to do was say nothing and I would lie in my bed at night, trembling. Can you explain that, Levy? I would lie awake praying that he would beat me instead, smash me with that fist, flay my back with his belt rather than that love, that silent displeasure. To please him, I learned whole passages of the Bible by heart; your Bible, Levy.'

"He tapped his whip against the top of his boots.

" 'Tell me, Levy. . . .'

" 'Yes, sir?'

"I know the Jews; a gentle people. Tell me honestly. Did your father ever beat you?'

" 'No, sir.'

" 'Not once?'

" 'Never, sir.'

" 'A gentle people, as I've said, but lax in your education, wouldn't you say?'

" 'Yes, sir.'

" 'Well, then we must remedy that.' "

Willi relit his cigar, took a puff, and left it in the ashtray. "I stood at attention all afternoon. He whipped me across the back until I learned the Ten Commandments by heart, and could repeat them word for word at his command: 'I am the Lord thy God, which have brought thee out of the land of Egypt, out of the house of bondage.' 'Thou shalt not!' 'Thou shalt not!' Thou shalt not!' "

Helene bit into an apple and looked at her watch. Danny shook his head.

"Never mind," she told him. "It's late. Past ten. Time for bed."

"Ten?" I repeated, standing up. "I've got to go myself."

"You w-w-w-wanna hear my r-r-record?" he asked me. "It'll only t-t-take a minute."

"O.K., for a minute."

His room was at the head of the stairs. I followed him up and he shut the door.

"Y-you never heard about H-H-Heinz before?"

"Never."

"I have. It gives me b-bad dreams."

On top of his desk was a phonograph record. He put it on the portable phonograph that stood in one corner of the room. For a time, sitting on the bed while the boy put on his pajamas, I listened to the deep voice chanting in the unintelligible tongue.

"D-don't you understand?"

"Not much," I said.

"How-how come you were never B-B-Bar Mitzvahed?"

"I wasn't as lucky as you. My father was dead, and my mother didn't care one way or the other."

"M-Mama doesn't care either," he said, tying his bathrobe around his waist. He rejected the record and stood by the window that faced the rose garden, biting his thumbnail.

"D-d-do you believe in G-G-God?"

"I don't know."

"I do-do."

"You're lucky there too."

"D-don't you ever pray?"

"No."

"I d-d-do, often."

I imagined that, rather like his laughter, that too must have been a wonderful relief; praying in silence, grateful and convinced that he was able to communicate something without a stutter.

"D-d-do you know what I p-pray for?" he asked me.

"What?"

"A-actually it's a s-s-secret."

"You can tell me if you like."

"S-sometimes, y-you know, when I think of all th-those people at the Temple—at the B-B-Bar Mitzvah, I mean—I get into a sweat."

"It'll be all right."

"There'll be h-hundreds of people there, M-Mama's whole family, G-G-Goldman's parents, and all his family, and all their f-f-friends."

"Who's Goldman?"

"He's a f-f-fink. Sammy Goldman. We're being B-B-Bar Mitzvahed together. He's rich. His father owns a chain of delicatessens. He's t-told everybody about me. He didn't want to g-go with me. He has p-pimples from p-p-playing with himself."

"It's late," I told him. "I really ought to go."

"It's another m-m-month or so. More. Time enough. Anything can h-h-happen in time, don't you think?"

"It depends."

"If you b-b-believe enough?"

"Maybe so."

"The st-st-stammer, you know, is all psychological. Doctor Rhinehart says so. It c-came all of a sudden. W-when I started school."

"I didn't know."

"Oh yes. And if it c-c-came that way, it can g-g-go too; suddenly, I mean. That's l-l-logical, don't you think?"

"Anything is possible," I told him.

He smiled abruptly, and opened his mouth again, giving me the impression that he wanted to say something more. But for some reason, maybe because he was tired, he got stuck; his chin jerked spasmodically as he tried to force the word from his mouth, and then he shrugged and gave up.

"Good luck," I told him.

One morning about a week later his father gave me a ring. He had a customer in the garment district, on Seventh Avenue and Thirty-seventh Street, and he thought that if as usual I was going to be working at the Forty-second Street Library, we could meet for lunch. I said fine. It was a hot day. We had a sandwich and a soda at Schrafft's and then he walked me back to the library, where we sat for a while on the granite steps under the trees around the flagpole at the north entrance on the avenue. The stairs were jammed with shopgirls and clerks taking in the sun before they had to go back to work.

"How's the work?" Willi asked me.

"Coming along. How's the family?"

"Fine. They send their best."

"Send my love."

"I will." He smoked a cigar and coughed. The air was thick with exhaust fumes. "You know, Danny doesn't say much, but he can't fool me."

"About what?"

"He's worried about the Bar Mitzvah. Speaking in front of all those people. I told him to take it slow and everything would be all right. What do you think?"

"You know best."

"Helene thinks I'm doing the wrong thing."

"It's not for me to say."

"Heinz taught me to love the Law. How he hated it! The Law is a yoke; it subdues the beast in us. I want Danny to love the Law too. I always demand too much of him. I told him yesterday to forget the service in the Temple. We'll just have a party at home."

"What'd he say?"

"Nothing doing. He wants to speak."

I spent the weekend of the Fourth with an ex-classmate and his wife at their cottage on the Cape. I got back Monday night. The service was scheduled for the following Saturday. I phoned Willi to make sure that it was on.

"You bet," he said. "You know, I think I've got a budding rabbi on my hands."

"How do you mean?"

"Danny gets up at six every morning to pray."

I bought him a series-E savings bond for twenty-five dollars plus fourteen silver dollars (one extra for good luck), and packed them in a velvet box with a clasp.

Saturday was hot and muggy. The service began at ten A.M. at Temple Shalom, on Seventy-eighth Avenue in Queens. I got there at a quarter of and chatted outside with Helene's sister and brother-in-law, who was a chiropodist from Brooklyn. He said, "I never thought Danny would go through with it."

The Goldmans drove up in a blue Caddy. Willi and his family arrived on foot. Danny was pale. He pulled my sleeve, and asked, "D-d-d-do you think they'll l-l-laugh?"

"Of course not."

"I p-p-prayed and p-p-prayed."

We sat together in the front pew, to the left of the Ark. Two big baskets of red roses were on the marble steps. A young rabbi, who was prematurely gray, conducted the morning service. Danny, on my right, picked his cuticles. Willi and Mr. Goldman held the Torah above the congregation and opened it on the podium. The Goldman kid recited his portion of the Haftorah first. His father, seated on the bimah between Willi and the rabbi, beamed at the crowd. Danny stood up. He mounted the three marble steps. The Goldman kid had evidently spread the word about Danny's stammer: the crowd was too quiet. Willi examined his fingernails. Danny looked at him, bowed his head, and spoke.

ISRAEL DURING
THE EICHMANN TRIAL:
A JOURNAL

Jerusalem
27 March 1961

Dinner at the Café Vienna, an expensive restaurant on Jaffa Road. Steak, greasy french fries. While I'm having coffee, in walks a bearded Moroccan beggar; his feet are wrapped in burlap sacks, tied with string. As is customary in this country, no one stops him from schnorring. He shuffles from one customer to the other at the espresso bar and everybody drops a few coins into his palm. Then a man wearing a Tyrolean hat, with a red feather, shouts in Hebrew, "Get away from me!"

The beggar says, "You don't have a Jewish heart."

My waiter later tells me, "The one wearing the hat was two years in Auschwitz."

28 March 1961

A joke going around town is that Eichmann will be condemned to live in Israel as a new immigrant without protekzia (i.e., "pull"—having the right connections).

The above from Shlomo Rosenberg, from whom I rent a room in his flat on Shamai Street.

Two months ago, while serving on *miloim,* or reserve duty in the army, he got into a discussion about Eichmann with a new immigrant, a Moroccan Jew, who said that if he had the chance, he'd cut Eichmann's throat.

Shlomo asked him, "Why? You haven't suffered from the Nazis. What have you got against Eichmann?"

"He didn't finish the job."

"What are you talking about?"

"Killing all the Ashkenazim."

It was a joke, Shlomo tells me, and yet . . . it expresses the trouble here between the Western and Oriental communities. The Moroccan doesn't like Ashkenazim "because they're the bosses."

28 March 1961

The country is getting ready for Passover. The restaurants are already serving matzos instead of bread.

"Jews pursue justice"—a Hebrew saying. Shula, Rosenberg's wife, tells me that she spent this afternoon at the opening session of a three-day conference on the Bible. It celebrates the 2500th anniversary of the Return from the Babylonian Captivity. The conference has two topics: the character of Cyrus, the Babylonian king who permitted the Jews to return here, then rebuild the Temple and Biblical "literature of wisdom"—like the Book of Job. The place was jammed; special rows of seats were reserved for soldiers.

Ben-Gurion lectured on King Cyrus. Most of the speakers were also not professional scholars, but writers, civil servants, accountants, etc., who love the Bible and study it in their spare time.

The lecture that caused the biggest stir was given by a young poet named Yitzkhak Shalev, who spoke on the Book of Job. Shalev argues that Job's acceptance of his fate is un-Jewish. Shalev says that Jews are on an eternal quest for an explanation of human suffering; we demand that suffering be deserved, and justice done.

Shula says the quest for justice is only one aspect of Jewish thought. More prominent is a passive, willful acceptance of suffering. She cites Maimonides: man cannot hope to know the answer; he must accept life the way it is and praise God.

Born in Poland in 1935, Shula spent the war hidden in a convent. She and her mother were the only members of her family who survived. She says, "I'm an atheist. I can't believe the Shoah is part of a divine plan."

2 April 1961

Pesach at Kibbutz Mizra, near Nazareth. I'm with my buddy Paul Danaceau, who's reporting the Eichmann trial on radio for Westinghouse. Perhaps eight hundred people are at the Seder, which is held in the communal dining hall. The tables are set with bottles of sweet red wine and orange juice, along with plastic plates heaped with cold chicken, chopped liver, and matzos. Because this is a holiday, families eat together. The kids squirm. Two accordionists, wearing embroidered Russian peasant blouses, play a medley of Israeli songs. Everybody sings "Hava Nagila."

The settlement's fat cultural director yells, "Sheckit!" ("Silence!"), and the Seder gets under way.

The Hagaddah is not the traditional one, but a variant published for the use of kibbutzim that belong to the Hashomer Hatzair, a left-wing Zionist movement. Excerpts from the Song of Songs ("the voice of the turtle is heard in our land"), then poems by Ibn Ezra, Bialik, and Shlonsky are read aloud. All the poetry celebrates the coming of spring, the end of the rainy season, planting crops, etc. Six girls dance in a circle.

The crowd chatters while a chorus of nine-year-olds asks the Four Questions. We eat the roast chicken, on which the fat is congealed. The wine bottles are left almost full.

One of the settlement's founders, a government minister in his sixties, memorializes Israeli soldiers who died in the War of Independence and the Sinai Campaign. "Remember all those who fell in battle! Their sacrifice redeemed us!"

A chorus sings the "Song of the Fighters of the Warsaw Ghetto," which the poet Shlonsky translated from Yiddish into Hebrew.

"We celebrate our fighters. My father was gassed at Auschwitz, and my brother Aaron was killed in Jerusalem during the War of Liberation. I mourn for both, but I'm proud of Aaron, who died like a soldier, with a gun in his hands."

This from Moshe, a kibbutz member, on my left, who fought with the British Army in North Africa and Italy during the Second World War.

He admits the new Hagaddah is not completely satisfactory.

"Yes," I tell him. "Something is missing. It lacks unity."

He says, "It lacks God. Say it! God is not a dirty word. We don't praise God. That's what's missing."

8 April 1961

Jerusalem is crawling with reporters from all over the world. Dinner at the Hungarian restaurant on King George Street; a party of German journalists is at the next table. The boss, who escaped from Budapest just before the Nazis marched in, apologizes to the Germans because he has no bread—only matzos—to serve with the meal.

Peter Atwanya, a Nigerian reporter, tells me that the trial has great significance for Africans. "South Africa is just as bad as Nazi Germany—the same system—with secret police, concentration camps, forced labor. Someday the world will know about it. The Jews have shown the way. We'll have our own trials. Wait and see."

He's staying at the King David. He says he can't eat in the dining room because people stare at him. He has his meals sent up to his room.

There is so much talk about Eichmann that a story making the rounds concerns the muhktar of an Arab village, who doesn't know who Eichmann is, and wants to rename a street after him to ingratiate himself with the Jews.

10 April 1961
10:45 P.M.
The trial begins at 9 A.M. tomorrow. Tonight, as usual, the streets are deserted, recalling the joke about the Englishman who served five years in the Palestine constabulary. When he visited Jerusalem after 1948, he asked why the curfew was still in effect.

12 April 1961
Talks with reporters. This afternoon, with a bald German, who's covering the trial for a West Berlin newspaper. Our mutual friend Ali, a Turkish reporter for the *Tanin Journal*, tried twice to introduce us, but the German politely excused himself and walked away. Today, in the pressroom, he offered me a cigarette and asked, "What do you make of it?"

I shrugged. He said, "Yes, what can one say?"

"How long will you stay?"

"Three weeks, perhaps, not more. There's no real interest in the trial in Germany, no matter what the authorities claim."

"What about the young people?"

"They don't care. They're innocent. What do they have to do with the guilt of the older generation? Men like Eichmann aren't just a German problem. You Americans have military leaders like him. How about those generals who ordered the bomb dropped on Hiroshima?"

14 April 1961

Shlomo Rosenberg asks me if Eichmann looks bloodthirsty.
"Absolutely not."
"Like Ari," he says.
"Who's Ari?"
"My army friend. A kid with freckles. We fought in Sinai together in 1956. He carried a red fire ax in his backpack from Tel Aviv and used it in hand-to-hand combat at El Arish. He doesn't look like he enjoys chopping people up."

15 April 1961

The newsmen talk a lot about Eichmann's ordinary appearance. Late this afternoon, in the pressroom, a Dane was reminded of what happened in his country during the Occupation. "We wanted to believe that the Germans weren't human. But they were. Most were ordinary people, like ourselves."

A young German reporter says, "No!"

I run into him a few minutes later on the stairs. His name is Gerhardt; he's covering the trial for two Bavarian papers. "I'm twenty-one years old," he says. "This is one of the most important experiences of my life."

We walk up King David Road toward the King David Hotel. He says, "I'm ashamed to be a German."

As a child of five, toward the end of the war, he witnessed the evacuation of Jews from a concentration camp outside his Bavarian village. "The Jews were driven through the main street with whips. That night I heard shots and screams from the forest. Everybody in town knew what was happening, but nobody protested. Why? We Germans are very brave. Why didn't we resist evil? Yesterday, in court, I saw a photograph of the corpse of a little boy at Belsen who had been tortured by the SS. They had put out one of his eyes."

Dinner at the Café Vienna with Lazar Rabinowitz, an Israeli lawyer, who survived the Vilna Ghetto and Auschwitz. He attends the trial every day. "In Vilna, the Germans issued labor cards to the heads of families of three or more people, which exempted only two from deportation. You had to choose. Write the truth about the Holocaust! We Jews were all forced by the Germans to become accomplices to our own murder."

16 April 1961

At My Bar, a joint popular with newsmen, the bartender told me that my German friend Gerhardt got drunk the other night and wept.

17 April 1961

In the pressroom this morning, Gerhardt said that another German reporter staying with him at the German hospice maintains that the Jews committed atrocities against the Arabs during the War of Independence.

"He told me they cut open pregnant women at Deir Yassin."

18 April 1961

At the Hebrew University with Bernard Casper, the dean of students. He wears a yarmulka. "The Holocaust will strengthen our faith in the Almighty," he says. "Jewish belief is best expressed in the words with which Job dismisses the consolations of his comforters: 'Though He slay me, yet will I trust in Him.'"

I told this to Shula, who laughed.

Spent this evening in the home of Shoshanna Raziel, the widow of the founder of the Irgun, who was killed fighting for the British in Iraq in 1941. She's about forty-five; stout, prematurely wrinkled.

She listens with great interest to all the broadcasts of the trial and for the first time realizes that there is something to Eichmann's defense that he was only following orders. "In the underground here, during the Mandate, I often ordered people to do things that would be inconceivable in normal times."

She also said, "Our claim to be the Chosen People is the cause of anti-Semitism.

"We must renounce such craziness. We Jews aren't special. We're like everybody else. A light unto the Gentiles? Foolishness! If that were true, we wouldn't try Eichmann. We'd let him go."

She showed me the 9-mm Parabellum pistol that her husband, David, gave her on her sixteenth birthday.

19 April 1961

Spicy goulash for lunch at the Hungarian restaurant on King George Street. Zolly, the boss, points out the pretty blond eating with two captains in the Israeli army. After they leave, Zolly says, "I knew her in Budapest. Eichmann deported her to Auschwitz in May 1944. She was sixteen; a great beauty! An SS doctor sterilized her, and she was forced to work in a Wehrmacht brothel, with 'Nur für Offiziere'—'Only for officers'—tattooed on her belly."

20 April 1961

Independence Day. At the parade with Leonard Fein, an American Jew who's doing research on Israeli politics. He was proud of the marching paratroopers, roaring tanks, and weapon carriers. Yet his favorite Jewish joke is about the Russian Jew who was drafted into the army during the Russo-Japanese War, given a rifle, and sent to the front.

His officer commands him: "Fire!"

"Fire? Are you crazy?" says the Jew. "There are people out there!"

26 April 1961

Dreamed last night I was a prisoner in Auschwitz; an SS man cut off my nose with a garden shears.

5 May 1961

Martin Buber. His shaggy white mustache and beard hide his mouth. Unable to read his lips, I have trouble understanding his thick German accent.

He looks in my eyes the whole time.

He asks, "How old are you?"

"Twenty-eight."

"Don't try to grasp the meaning of the evil revealed at the trial with your rational mind alone."

I start scribbling down his words. "Please don't," he says. "I want you to speak to me, as well as listen.

"We Jews do not admit a dualistic explanation of evil. We don't believe in Satan. God has a demonic aspect. 'I make peace, and create evil,' says God, according to the prophet Isaiah. So it seems that the Almighty Himself attacks us, makes us accomplices to our own destruction—as in your friend's story of the labor card.

"Man was created with a will of his own so that he may oppose God. That's the mystery! Like Jacob, we must wrestle with God for His blessing.

"For that, we need two things: the faith of Job, who says—"

" 'Even though He slay me, yet will I trust in Him.' "

Buber says, "Very good! But what else do we need, do you know?"

"No."

"A sense of humor!"

I ask, "Would you condemn Eichmann to death?"

He says no. "I do not believe that executing him is worthy of Israel's transcendent destiny: being a light unto the nations.

"But Israel has re-entered history. This country is struggling to re-establish its nationhood. In order to survive, it is absorbed with specific political, social, economic, and military problems. Indifferent for the moment to its spiritual mission, it will in time be true to itself and wrestle again with God. Many of its young people, like yourself, have already assumed this burden. Even now, the wrestling goes on in them, as it does in you and me."

THE PRISONER

In the winter of 1906, when my father was fourteen years old, the Russian military barracks on Mila Street in Warsaw was turned into a prison. The iron gate, with its crest of the two-headed eagle, became known in Polish as "The Portal of Tears," because it was from here that those prisoners convicted by military tribunal of having taken part in the uprising the year before were sent to the penal camps in Siberia, or the mines.

Late one night after the first of the year, one of the prison's turnkeys, a Pole who had been bribed by the congregation of the neighborhood synagogue, came across the street and knocked three times on my grandfather's door.

"Who is it?" the boy called out.

"Open up."

"Who's there?"

"Ha Malach," the Pole had been taught to reply to identify himself—in Hebrew, "the angel," literally "the messenger," one who has been sent from God—so that when the boy opened the door the dark figure in the overcoat and fur cap set his heart to pounding, and made him catch his breath.

"Is his honor at home?"

"Who?"

"Your father, quick! Where is he?"

"In the kitchen," the boy told him. "Come in."

The meeting had been arranged months before, at the beginning of the summer, in the event that a Jew should be imprisoned at the barracks.

"Go to bed, David," his father said.

"Have they really got a Jew? Will you go and see him?"

The Pole raised his head in the flickering candlelight and grinned.

Ha Malach. . . . A messenger from God who wears a fur cap. Is that possible? the boy wondered the next morning as he wound his phylacteries around his arm to pray. Through the frosted window above his bed he could see the sentries marching up and down. He tried to picture the Jewish prisoner in his cell. Israel in Egypt, Joseph in the dungeons of the Pharaoh: all those he had read about who had suffered torture and martyrdom for the Sanctification of the Name ran through his mind. He felt exhausted and feverish. All night long, he had dreamed of smoldering faggots and bloody whips. What if he were called upon one day to help a captive? Would he prove worthy of the holy obligation?

"Hineni," he prayed aloud in Hebrew. "Here I am. Lord God of my Fathers, Master of the Universe, do with me what you will."

"Is it true? Are you going to the barracks?" he asked his father at breakfast.

"On Friday, yes. He wants a blanket and some food."

"But what about the guards?" asked the boy, buttering his bread.

"The guards can be bribed."

"For how much?"

"Fifty rubles."

"Fifty rubles! Where will you get fifty rubles?"

"Where do you think? From the synagogue, of course."

And so it was. Night after night, for the remainder of the week, the old man passed the hat in the vestibule of the synagogue up the street.

"Five kopeks?" he shouted at Rabinowitz the cobbler. "Five miserable kopeks is all you can spare for a scholar who once studied Torah with the Sage of Kotsk?"

"The Sage of where?" asked Jacobson the hatmaker.

"Yes, it's true. With Rabbi Getz of Kotsk himself," said Bunem the sexton, who cleared his throat, and in his high, piping voice read aloud from a letter that the rabbi had addressed to the whole congregation:

"Is it true what I have heard? Avram Shulmann? Condemned

to seven years? Surely our brothers in Warsaw will find it in their hearts to do whatever they can for one whom I had once hoped would teach the Law in my place when I am gone."

"Condemned for seven years?" repeated the cobbler.

"Yes, and to the mines! To the lead mines, Jews, do you hear?" cried Bunem, snatching the hat and shoving it under Rabinowitz's nose.

"But for what? What's he done?" the boy wanted to know. Nobody answered. It didn't make sense. Not if the prisoner had studied with the Sage of Kotsk. Not unless . . . The boy gaped at his father counting the coins in the hat. Unless—may God forbid —he had denied the Almighty, and become an anarchist or a socialist of some kind, one of those wild young men who threw bombs at the police and erected barricades on Market Street.

There were all sorts of rumors about him, whispered in the back of the synagogue, or on the steps outside: he had been a Kabbalist, an ascetic mystic, who was forced to leave Kotsk after a young girl, practically a child, had hanged herself in the House of Study.

"Nonsense," said the cantor, after services on Thursday night, when the fifty rubles had been collected. He swore that the sister of the cantor of Kotsk, his wife's cousin, had written him the truth. The prisoner had gone mad after a pogrom in the town some years ago, and tearing off his clothes in the marketplace, had denied God and attacked the rabbi with his nails and teeth.

"Stark raving mad," said the cantor. "It's a fact."

When his father returned from the barracks just before sundown the next night, the boy was completely bewildered. "What happened? Did you see him?" he asked.

"Yes, I saw him," said the old man.

"What did he say?"

"He thanked me for the blanket and the roast."

"Is that all?"

"What else did you expect?"

"But you were there the whole afternoon."

The old man washed his hands and slipped into a clean caftan for the Sabbath meal.

"Eat, Mikhal," his wife coaxed him at the table. "The soup will get cold."

"What? Oh yes, the soup," he replied, putting down his spoon to rise abruptly from the table and take his Bible down from the shelf.

"What is it, Papa? What's the matter?" asked the boy.

"Nothing."

But it was a lie. For half the night, until he fell into a dreamless sleep, the boy heard him pace the floor, pausing now and then to mutter some passage in Hebrew under his breath. In the morning, he sat in front of the kitchen window, staring at the huge dark building across the street, with the Bible closed in his lap.

"What did he say?" the boy repeated. "Has he become a socialist? Is that the trouble?"

"Who told you that?"

"Is it true?"

"Yes" said the old man.

"Then he doesn't believe in God?"

The old man laughed and said, "Oh yes, he believes."

The boy couldn't figure it out. On Tuesday night, the Pole knocked on the door again, and insisted on seeing the old man, who had already gone to bed. They spoke in the kitchen behind a closed door.

The door was then flung open. Once again, the man in the fur cap with the long mustache filled the boy with the same feelings —exaltation and dread. His mouth was dry.

"Where're you going?" he called out to his father.

"He wants to see me."

"At this hour?"

"I'll be back as soon as I can. Tell your mother," said the old man, putting on his shoes. On the kitchen table lay the opened Bible. The boy examined the yellowed pages. A passage from Hosea had been underlined by the imprint of his father's fingernail.

" '. . . I will be like a lion to them,' " he read aloud. " 'Like a leopard will I lurk by the way. I will meet them like a bear who has lost her clubs, and tear open their breasts. There will I devour them like a lion. Like a wild beast will I rend them. . . .' "

What did it mean? It was a passage the boy had never understood. This was the Lord of the Universe who was speaking, the God of Mercy who was comparing Himself to a wild animal stalking his prey. The fire in the stove went out. Shivering, the boy fell asleep with his head on his arm.

For the next two days, his father shuffled around the house in his felt slippers. The boy had never seen him pray with such fervor. In the evenings, particularly, just before he went to bed, he finished with trembling lips and tears in his eyes. The Bible remained open on the kitchen table. "Impossible," he muttered through clenched teeth, reading the same passage again and again. "Impossible. . . . What does he want from me?"

On Friday morning, he called his son to his room.

"Tell Bunem I want to see him," he said in a hoarse voice.

"What about me, Papa? Isn't there anything I can do?"

"Bunem," the old man insisted, and an hour or so later, when the boy had brought the sexton home, he lingered in the room in order to hear what his father had to say.

"Sit down. Sit down." He waved his hand. "A little brandy? No? Then sit a minute. I . . ." He lowered his eyes and the color rushed into his wrinkled cheeks. "You must . . . I . . . You must do me a favor," he went on at last.

"Of course."

"Yes. Very special. You must make him understand. I talk and I talk, but it doesn't do any good. He thinks . . . I have a message for him, for our friend, do you understand?"

"A message?" repeated the sexton in his high voice.

"You must tell him that I'm very sorry, but there's absolutely nothing I can do. Will you remember that?"

"I don't understand."

"It's very simple. All you have to do is repeat what I'm telling you."

"When?"

"This afternoon. I promised that I'd return today, but it's useless. Worse. You must go instead. Stanislaw will be here at five."

"Stanislaw?" said Bunem, rising to his feet.

"The turnkey. What's the matter with you?"

"B-but that's impossible," the sexton stammered. "W-what I mean to say is that I'd like to, of course—you know I would—but it's absolutely out of the question. A message! Are you mad? What about the police? What would happen to me if they found out I was giving information to a political prisoner?"

"The message is personal. You have nothing to fear from that."

"That's all very well for you to say with a grown son, practically a man who can look after himself if anything should happen to you —may God forbid! But what about my daughters? Three helpless girls. Who would look after them if anything happened to me? No. For their sake, I can't even think of taking such a chance." He shook his head. "B-but I'll tell you what I'll do. They can cook, those girls. Especially Leah. A roast chicken, how's that? And with potato pancakes. What do you say to that, eh?" He backed away toward the door. "And out of my own pocket. A whole roast chicken, a Sabbath feast for him to remember for the rest of his life, no matter what they do to him. Well? What do you say?"

"Tell Rabinowitz and Jacobson I want to see them," the old man answered, shutting his eyes.

He might as well have saved his breath. No one came except Leah, a good half a head taller than her father, with a deeper voice, and a prominent adam's apple like an adolescent boy, who brought the promised chicken and pancakes wrapped in a greasy newspaper. When she left, the boy waited in the kitchen for the turnkey's knock on the door.

"No, I won't go," his father repeated to himself under his breath, wandering around the house in his slippers.

"But what about the food?" the boy asked.

"The food?"

"The Pole will only eat it himself. It's not fair. The Sabbath is coming."

"The food, yes," said his father, sitting down with his head in his hands.

"Let me take it," said the boy.

"That's out of the question."

"Why? The guards have been bribed. It's perfectly safe. What would they want with me?"

"No," said his father.

There were three knocks on the door. Before his father had a chance to say anything more, the boy grabbed the greasy package from the table and ran into the hall.

"What is it now? Who are you?" asked the prisoner when the turnkey had locked the boy in the cell.

As far as he could make out, he was in a cellar of some kind, in one of the rooms off a long corridor with a vaulted ceiling that ran beneath a wing of the barracks that faced the inner court. "Who's there?" the prisoner repeated, with a rattle of chains. It was too dark for the boy to see his face. Without a window in the cell, it was already night in here, bitter cold, and yet stifling from a stench of excrement that had first stunned the boy when he and the Pole were only halfway down the last flight of stairs.

"I . . . That is, my father couldn't come," said the boy.

"Who?"

"My father. He said . . . I've brought you some food instead."

"How nice. That's very thoughtful. Thank you very much."

"Don't mention it. Good Shabbes," said the boy, handing him the package.

"By all means. And to you, too."

The boy's eyes were gradually becoming accustomed to the dark. He could see that the prisoner's head was shaved, cropped to the skull, and he was wearing a peculiar vest, like a uniform, with black and gray horizontal stripes.

"My father sends you a message," the boy went on.

"Oh?"

"He wanted me to tell you that he can't help you. There's nothing he can do."

"I see."

"But he says that he's very sorry."

"Yes, I understand. Will you thank him for me just the same?"

"Of course."

"Good."

Again there was the rattle of chains. The boy realized that the prisoner's wrists were chained to a thick leather strap around his waist. He squatted down on a pile of straw.

"What's your name?" the prisoner asked.

"David."

"Then David, do you know why I'm here?"

"I think so. You're a socialist."

"Do you know what that means?"

"I'm not sure. Did you throw a bomb?"

"Oh no, much worse. I wrote a book."

"About what?"

"About a lot of things. About a pogrom, a little girl, and the class struggle. Do you know what the class struggle is?"

"No."

"It's a war. A war against the Tsar, and the Cossacks, and the police. Against all the people who make pogroms. In a way, you know, I'm a soldier. But it's your war too."

"If you say so," said the boy.

"But it is. It's everybody's war, whether they like it or not, and it will go on and on for a long time to come. That's the rule of life. Can you keep a secret?"

"Yes."

"Would you like to do something for me? Something very important?"

"If I can."

"Do you know where Iron Street is?"

"I think so."

"Do you think you could find Number Twelve for me?"

"I could try. Why?"

"Shhh! Listen!"

"I don't hear anything."

"Yes, shhh!" the prisoner whispered. "The turnkey will be back in a moment, so there's no time to explain. Will you go to Number Twelve Iron Street on Sunday morning and deliver a very important message for me?"

"Yes," said the boy.

"Without telling another soul?"

"If that's what you want."

"That's very important. You must be careful. I'm relying on you because there's no one else I can ask."

"I understand."

"Good. At Number Twelve, you must knock three times on the porter's door, and a girl will answer, a Polish girl, with very blond hair and blue eyes. Her hair is almost white. You can't mistake her."

"What do I tell her?"

"You must say that you have a message from her cousin, who says that he's going away to the country at the end of next week, probably Friday. Can you remember all of that?"

"Yes."

"Fine. But you must promise to be as careful as you can. It's very dangerous. If anyone else answers the door, for example, you must say that you've made a mistake and go away."

"I'll remember."

"Good boy," said the prisoner. "Now tell me something."

"What?"

"How old are you?"

"Fourteen."

"Really? How strange. She was almost fourteen too."

"Who?"

"Yes, just about the same age. How strange," said the prisoner, in a distracted, dreamy voice, as the key turned suddenly in the lock, and the Pole threw open the door, lighting up the cell with the hurricane lamp he held in his hand.

The boy gave a start. The prisoner's face seemed to leap out of the dark. Because of his shaved head, his ears stuck out, and his eyes looked enormous. He blinked painfully, and tried to raise his hands, rattling his chains.

"I gave him your message," the boy told his father when he got home. "He said to thank you."

The old man nodded and looked away.

On Sunday morning, the boy woke to the peal of church bells, and stumbled into the empty kitchen for a glass of tea. Iron Street, Number Twelve. A blond Polish girl, with blue eyes. What was she like, he wondered, tiptoeing to the front door. Did she actually smoke like some of the girls—students, socialists, God only knew what—whom he often saw in the cafés on Marshalkovska Street, puffing away on yellow Russian cigarettes? Was she also wanted by the police for writing books? And if they caught her, would they shave off her hair?

"David?"

"I'll be back in a little while, Papa."

"Come in here a moment. Where are you going at this hour?"

"Nowhere, Papa. Just out for a walk."

"At this hour? Come in here, I say."

The boy did as he was told. His mother was still in bed. Already dressed and preparing to begin his morning prayers, the old man questioned his son again. On the dresser beside him, bound in black, was a prayer book with the morning service containing the words from the psalm that the boy knew by heart: ". . . deliver my soul, O God, from lying lips and from a deceitful tongue. . . ."

"Well?" said the old man, waiting for an answer.

The boy told him the truth. "But I was doing it for you, too, after all."

"What are you talking about?" said his father.

"Didn't he ask you to go to Iron Street?"

"Is that what he told you? Where's my coat?" the old man shouted.

"Where are you going?"

"My coat!"

The boy followed him outside. It had begun to snow. They crossed the street, went through the gate past the yawning sentries and down the cellar stairs, into the dark, vaulted corridor, where the astonished Pole dropped an armful of straw to open up the prisoner's cell.

"Yes, what of it?" he admitted to the old man. "I found out when I was to be deported, and the Party had to be informed."

"At the risk of a child's life?"

"Yes."

"And if he'd been caught?"

"Then whatever he would have suffered would have been meaningful, at least; to some end."

"The Revolution?"

"Yes."

"Which alone can give meaning to human suffering?"

"By making an end to it, yes," said the prisoner. His face was turned away, hidden by darkness, but from the sound of his voice, the boy had the impression that his eyes were tightly shut.

"I don't understand, Papa. What does he mean?"

"Tell him," said the prisoner. "He has a right to judge for himself."

The old man remained silent.

"Then listen to me," the prisoner went on, grabbing the boy by the arm. "I told you, it's a war . . . for you . . . for the children, the little girl, remember? Fourteen years old, your age, with long black hair. . . . When I was studying Torah with Rabbi Getz at Kotsk, there was a pogrom. One Sunday, after church, the police gave the peasants brandy. On orders from the district commissioner himself. There was a drought that season, and the crops had failed. The peasants were starving. 'Turn them on the Jews' was the order. The police gave them brandy, and they murdered the Jews. The rabbi and I hid in the attic of the House of Study where all the old prayer books were stored, piles of them, loose pages by the thousands, turning yellow, gnawed by mice and crumbling to dust. We buried ourselves alive under books, listening to the screams. I raised my head to the window.

" 'Don't look,' the rabbi tells me. 'Shut your eyes, my son, and pray.'

"But I look just the same. I can't tear my eyes away, so I see what they do to a fourteen-year-old girl, the daughter of the Jew who owns the mill on the edge of town. One of them sits on her head, while they take turns. All told, there are six of them, and when they're finished, and see that she's still alive, still fully conscious, they cut open her belly with a sickle, and stuff it with goose feathers from a pillow they've looted from a house across the street.

" 'Don't look,' the rabbi tells me, 'don't look.' But it was too late. I had seen everything . . . the whole truth."

"The truth?" the boy repeated.

"It's a war," said the prisoner, rattling his chains. "A war."

When the old man and the boy left the cell, the Pole followed them to the gate.

"Can I help your honor?" he asked, shivering in his cotton blouse. The boy had become accustomed to him. He was now just an ordinary man, with eyes watering from the cold. Yet, because of the falling snow, there was something mysterious about the whole scene. It was as if the invisible were on the verge of becoming visible before the boy's eyes. Yes, that was it, exactly, thought the boy. It was because of the air. The thick, feathery snowflakes imparted a visible depth to the air—something the boy had never noticed before; it frightened him.

"Go home, David," said his father. "Tell Mama I'll be back as soon as I can."

He walked off, through the gate, heading toward the Prospect. To Iron Street? The boy never found out. And did the Pole, too, suspect something of the kind? He wiped his running eyes. Who could tell what he was thinking? He came to the house twice more, on Monday and Thursday of the following week, to persuade the old man to see the prisoner for the last time.

"What does he want from me now?" he asked, closing his Bible.

"He says your honor already knows."

"Then I can do nothing for him. No, nothing," he repeated to his son. "You needn't look at me like that. There's nothing that either you or I or anyone can do for him anymore, and that's all there is to it."

But on Thursday afternoon, as the boy knew he would, the old man relented. He and the boy followed the Pole through the gate for the last time, and down the steps to the cellar.

"It's happened again," said the prisoner, rising to his feet.

"When?"

"Twice so far this week. On Monday, and again this morning. And it's getting worse."

"How do you mean?"

"How can I explain? It's . . . The feeling is getting stronger, somehow, and it lasts longer. For minutes at a time."

"What's he mean, Papa? What's he talking about?" the boy asked.

"This morning, for example," said the prisoner. "I was lying here, thinking about the mines. That once I was there, everything would be all right. That is, there are Party cells out there, you know, even classes, and lectures from the Comrades, after a fashion, a whole organization under their very noses, so that you can carry on with the work that has to be done, and one needn't give up hope. The struggle goes on. . . ."

"And then what?" the old man interrupted him.

"I told you. Like before. The light. . . . It . . . It was breakfast time, and the turnkey opened the door to give me the bread. . . . I . . . It's hard to describe. His lamp, you know. For a moment, it blinds me. Afterwards, it takes a minute or so to get used to the dark again. That is, to see in the dark. Generally, I can see in here very well, but when he shines a light . . . Anyway, most of the time, I'm blind for a minute or two, and then it passes, and that's all there is to it. But this morning, like Monday, and as I've told you, three or four times before, it seemed more than just dark, more than just the absence of light, as if the darkness were a substance itself. . . . Yes . . . The same, as solid—or, rather, as fluid, or maybe gaseous, as that stone wall, for example; yes, as real as that, or the oak door. . . . Yet not exactly solid, either, or even like a gas—real, but not material at all. . . ."

He went on in a whisper. "No, maybe that's not the right word. It . . . I shut my eyes, tight, but it didn't do any good. When I opened them, it was worse. Darker, somehow, dissolving everything, the stone and the wood, or, rather, as if the dark and the stone and the wood were all the same. . . . Exactly. As if everything were part of everything else. . . . The floor, too, and the straw, and then my legs, my left one first, and then the other, and my hands, and the chains on my wrists, all dissolving. Everything on the verge of becoming a part of everything else. By this time, I could see again, perfectly: the straw on the floor, even the dirt under my fingernails, each and every straw, and every one perfectly distinct, and . . . significant. Meaningful, each one, every straw on the floor, the way it lay, either lengthwise or crosswise. It seemed right and good—morally good, you understand—that each one should be the way it was—perfect. In perfect order. . . . No. Much more than that. There was . . . joy."

"Joy," repeated the old man.

"And then, like before. Myself. My own body. Even the chains. Solid, material, and perfect, but then again, on the verge of dissolving too, trembling, like everything else, so that I had to hold myself in—my breath, with all the strength I had. . . . No, not my breath so much. More than that, much more. . . . My ruach. The Hebrew word describes it best. The breath and the spirit together. . . . I had to hold it back with all the strength I had, because it too seemed on the verge of becoming part of the rest . . . dissolved . . . with joy. If I let go, it would rush out, and merge . . . roar out. The prisoner's voice rose. "Roar with joy. . . .

"Joy! How could I? What about that child? Oh, I could remember it all, vividly: the dusty street, the peasant with the sunburned neck who held the sickle, the girl herself, her foot, with the shoe untied . . . but it was like the straws. All in order. The sickle, the untied shoe—everything. It was . . . good. No, holy."

"Let go of my arm," said the old man.

"Make Him stop," the prisoner said. "Hasn't He done enough?"

"Who, Papa? What is he talking about?" said the boy.

"Tell me how to make Him stop!" the prisoner cried.

"Let go of my arm," cried the old man. "Let me go!"

CHARITY

My mother died in the winter of 1912, when I was twelve years old. My parents and I lived in one room of a cold-water flat on Ludlow Street on Manhattan's Lower East Side. My father was a finisher of men's pants. He lined the pants at the waistline and hemmed the pockets. Working twelve hours a day on his rented Singer sewing machine, he made an average of seven dollars a week. My mother sewed on the buttons and buckles. When I got home from school, I delivered the finished pants to the subcontractor on Stanton Street who had hired us.

Our monthly rent was fourteen dollars. We ate a roll and a cup of chicory-flavored coffee for breakfast, a bowl of chicken soup for lunch, and a crust of rye bread and big green pickles for supper. I went to bed hungry. We splurged Friday nights in celebration of the coming of the Sabbath. As a religious Jew, my father insisted upon it. We scrimped and saved all week, and on Friday afternoons my mother went shopping on Hester Street, where she bought everything from the pushcart peddlers or the outdoor stalls.

When I got home on Friday afternoon, the table would already be set with a pair of brass candlesticks and chipped china plates with little rosebuds painted on them. There would be a fresh loaf of challah, covered by a threadbare embroidered doily, a little glass goblet of sweet red wine for each of us, a plate of stuffed carp, sweet-and-sour meat, roast potatoes saturated with gravy, and candied carrots. Soup—chicken soup again—made from legs and wings, always came last, and for dessert my mother would serve calf's-foot jelly, which she had cooked that afternoon and set out on the fire escape to cool. Mother would light the candles and pronounce the benediction over them, and after blessing the bread and wine, my father would turn to our guest and invite him to eat.

We always had a guest on Friday nights, someone poorer than we, who had no place to celebrate the Sabbath. It was a religious obligation. On Friday afternoons, my father took an hour off from work to wander the streets of the neighborhood, looking for a Jewish beggar or a starving Hebrew scholar who slept on the benches of some shul. They were almost always old men smelling of snuff, who wore ragged beards and earlocks, and had dirty fingernails.

Very often on particularly cold nights, my father invited them to remain with us. They slept on the floor, covered by a woolen blanket. Their snoring made it impossible for me to sleep.

"Papa," I'd complain.

"Shhh!" he'd tell me. "Remember. 'Charity saves from death.' "

He quoted the proverb from the Bible in Hebrew, and I shut up. I lay in the dark, listening to the snoring. The room was freezing. Coal was too expensive to keep the stove burning all night. Very often, in the mornings, the glass of water by my bed would be frozen solid.

My mother caught pneumonia in the middle of December. She awoke on a Wednesday, as I remember, about midnight, with a splitting headache and a severe chill that made her teeth chatter and a raging fever that for some reason flushed only the left side of her face. It looked as if she had been slapped. Every bone in her body ached, and within a few hours, at about two in the morning, she was suffering from an agonizing pain in her right side.

"Like a knife," she whispered through clenched teeth.

Convulsed by a short, dry cough, she lay in bed for two more days. The left side of her face was still flushed. She breathed very quickly, with a grunt every time she exhaled. When she drew a breath, her nostrils were distended. There were open sores on her upper lip. Her dark brown eyes were peculiarly bright—I had never seen them so beautiful. I wanted to kiss her quivering lips. But the barking cough made her raise herself up and claw at her right side. She began to spit blood.

In her semi-delirium, she babbled half-remembered legends

from her childhood, and things she had read in Yiddish chapbooks written for women.

"Is it snowing?" she asked me.

"Yes."

"Ah, but not there," she whispered. "Never there."

"Where?" my father asked her, and she gazed at him with her glittering eyes, and smiled. "Where do you think? Where there are fruit trees, trees with golden leaves, always in bloom. Apple trees and orange trees, and one huge tree, they say, where apples, oranges, pears, and grapes grow on the same branches, all together . . ."

He rubbed her moist, hot hands. "Listen to me. This kind of talk is forbidden. Forbidden, Malka, do you understand me? Can you hear me? It's absolutely forbidden to talk this way. One must want to live."

"I've been a good wife, haven't I?" she asked.

"Of course."

"I've tried. God knows, I've tried to be a good wife, a good mother, and a good Jew."

"Of course you have," my father said.

"I'm glad. I've read, you know, that when a righteous soul is about to enter Paradise, the angels come and strip off her shroud and dress her in seven robes woven from the clouds of glory. Did you know that? Seven shining robes. And on her head they put two crowns. One of gold and the other . . . I forget now what the other is."

My father yelled, "Stop it!"

When I came home that Friday afternoon, a doctor was there from the hospital on Second Avenue and Seventeenth Street. He was a tall German Jew who wore a blond goatee.

"Yes," he said in English, putting away his stethoscope. "The crisis will come in a week, maybe a little less."

"The crisis?" I repeated. "What's that?"

He stroked his goatee. "She'll get worse, and then, if she's strong enough, her fever will drop and she'll survive. Of course, she'd have a much better chance in the hospital."

"What's that?" my father asked in Yiddish. "What's he saying?"

"It's up to you," the doctor went on, addressing me. "But that's my considered professional opinion."

"A hospital?" my father suddenly repeated in English. It was the only word he had understood. He shook his head. "No!" His eyes filled with tears. I knew what he was thinking. In the shtetl north of Odessa from which he'd come, the hospital was a shack on the edge of town, supported by the local burial society, where the poor were sent to die.

My mother coughed. The doctor glanced at his gold watch and said, "Well?"

"This is America, Papa," I told him. "The doctor says that Mama will have a much better chance in the hospital."

The watch ticked, my mother gasped for breath, and my father nodded.

"Good," the doctor said. "I'll make the arrangements. The ambulance will be here in about an hour. In the meantime, keep her as warm as possible."

After I wrapped my mother in my own quilt, stuffed with goose feathers, my father said, "God forgive me. I almost forgot."

"What?"

"You'll have to do the shopping," he told me.

"For what?"

"For the Sabbath, what do you think?"

"Tonight?"

"The Sabbath is the Sabbath."

"I'm not hungry tonight."

"But our guest will be."

"Tonight?" I repeated.

"And why should tonight be different from last Friday night, or the Friday before that?"

My mother coughed again into her handkerchief. It was soaked with blood when she brought it away from her mouth.

"Listen to your father," she whispered.

"No."

"Do what he tells you," she said.

I went down to Hester Street, which was jammed with shoppers despite the bitter cold. I stopped in front of a pushcart peddler who sold cracked eggs at a penny apiece. Then, all at once, I understood. It was a *mitzvah* my father was performing, a good

deed, a holy act, which bound the upper and nether worlds, and
hastened the redemption of Israel. I glanced up at the low clouds,
which had a reddish glow, reflecting the lights below. It was a sign;
the heavens and the earth had come closer together. And tonight
of all nights, when it was a matter of life and death. The Holy One,
blessed be He, saw everything. My father's charity would not go
unrewarded. I walked on through the slush that seeped into my
shoes. Scrawny chickens and half-plucked geese hung by their feet
in a doorway, awaiting the butcher's knife. The butcher, covered
with feathers and spattered with blood, spat into the gutter, and
tested the blade of his knife on the ball of his thumb. It began to
snow.

By the time I reached home, my mother was gone, but there
with my father was a tall, emaciated, stoop-shouldered man wearing a ragged black frock coat and a battered black silk top hat.
Over one arm, he carried an umbrella.

"This is Reb Rifkin," said my father.

"I know. Good Shabbes."

"And a peaceful Sabbath to you, too," Rifkin answered me in his
high, cracked voice.

I had seen him around the neighborhood for years. He was a
broken-down Hebrew teacher who barely kept himself alive by
giving Hebrew lessons for ten cents apiece. He lived in a shul on
Essex Street, where he slept in a tiny unheated room behind the
Ark. It was said that a rat had bitten off one of his toes.

He warmed his blue hands over the coal stove while my father
and I prepared supper. Because the doctor had been so expensive
—two dollars—we had only a little chicken soup with noodles, half
a loaf of stale challah, the head of a carp, a bowlful of raisins and
almonds for dessert, and a glass of steaming tea with lemon. My
father gave Rifkin the fish head and he devoured everything except the eyes and the bones, which he sucked one by one.

"God bless you," he said, wiping his fingers on his beard. "Would
you believe it? Except for a little salted herring and a glass of tea,
this is the only thing I've had in my mouth for two days."

He had a tiny white spot on his right pupil which made him
seem unable to look you straight in the eye. He appeared to gaze
slightly above you and a little to the left.

"How's Mama?" I asked my father.

"In God's hands."

"How true. Aren't we all?" asked Rifkin. "If I hadn't gone for a walk on Ludlow Street and met you, I'd be in my room right now, lying in the dark. The rats eat my candles."

"When can we visit her?" I went on.

"Tomorrow."

"I heard the sad news," Rifkin said to me. "But don't you worry about a thing. God willing, she'll be well in no time."

"I hope so," my father said.

"How can you doubt it?" Rifkin cried out. "God is just, but He's merciful too. To whom will He not show His mercy if not to a fine woman like that and her husband who feeds the starving?"

"We shall see," my father said.

"Well, I should be going," said Rifkin, picking up his umbrella.

"Nonsense," my father said. "It's snowing. Stay the night and share breakfast with us tomorrow morning. Lunch and supper too, if you like. Whatever we have in the house."

"No, no, I couldn't think of it."

"But I insist."

"Well, of course, if you put it like that . . ."

Rifkin snored; not only snored, but whistled. I couldn't sleep, so I got up and with the blanket wrapped around my shoulders went out onto the landing. We lived on the fourth floor. The building reeked of urine from the toilets at the end of each hallway and the smell of cooked cabbage, fried onions, and fish. There was the whir of sewing machines. To make ends meet, God help us, some Jews were forced to work on the Sabbath. I sat down on the steps. The words of the proverb rang in my head: "Happy is he that hath mercy on the poor."

"Jacob, is that you?" my father whispered when I went back into the room.

"Yes, Papa."

"Are you all right?"

"Fine, Papa."

"Come over here a minute."

"What's the matter?"

"I can't sleep."

"Neither could I, but I feel much better now."

"Do you? Why?"

"Because Mama will get well."

"How can you be so sure?"

"You said so yourself."

"Did I? When?"

"You said that charity saves from death."

"What's that got to do with Mama?"

"Everything."

He suddenly raised his voice. "Is that what you think a mitzvah is? A bribe offered the Almighty?"

"But you said so. You said that charity saves from death." Rifkin groaned in his sleep.

"No, not Mama," my father said in a hoarse voice. "Him."

A PILE OF STONES

"Dear Milton," Nina writes.

> We had a tragedy a day or so after the card I sent you. Bill was
> drowned. He hadn't swum in the ocean for such a long time, he
> couldn't resist that treacherous water. The undertow knocked him
> off his feet, and up against some rocks. I know that you will be
> greatly saddened by the news.
>
> I am with his family in Greenwich for a few days. Then I will
> go back to my parents in New Canaan for the rest of the summer.
> After that, I'm not sure what I will do. Perhaps come to New York,
> and get my M.S. at the Columbia University School of Social Work.
> But I'm still terribly shocked. I just wanted to let you know, for I
> know that you loved him. . . .

I can't find the card. It was mailed about a week ago, from Bar
Harbor, where they had gone to spend the first two weeks of July.
According to Bill's last letter, written to me at the beginning of
May, they were going on vacation to celebrate his promotion. He
had just been made a full partner in his father's law firm in Stam-
ford, in charge of all the corporate litigation. It was his special
interest when I knew him at Yale Law School. And he was good
at it. Not brilliant, but hard-working, with something of a reputation on campus for being a grind.

It's one of the ways I remember him best: at two o'clock in the
morning, with his stockinged feet up on his desk, and a copy of
Wigmore on Evidence open in his lap, alternately taking a deep
drag from his cigarette and scribbling a note on the pad of lined

yellow paper fixed to the steel clipboard he always carried with him to class.

As far as I know, the only outside interest he had was a religious study group he had organized with five or six divinity students and two undergraduates who met twice a month, on Sundays, after morning services at a local Presbyterian church. Churchgoing for its own sake didn't particularly compel him. Sometimes he went, and sometimes he didn't. He never missed a meeting of the study group, though, and in the week before it met spent most of his spare time reading religious books. He pored through Tillich and Niebuhr, somebody or other by the name of Bonhoeffer, and, just after Thanksgiving, a writer, he said, who ought to interest me very much.

"Who's that?" I wanted to know.

"Martin Buber. We're having a discussion next Sunday on his interpretation of Hasidism. What's the matter? He's a great Jewish thinker. You ought to be very proud."

He showed me the photo of the bearded old man on the cover of the paperback edition of his *Tales of the Hasidim.*

"He looks like my grandfather."

"Then why don't you come on Sunday?" Bill said. "All we do is have brunch and sit around and talk. It's very informal. You might enjoy it."

"I'd like to, really, but I can't. I won't be here. I've got a date in New York on Saturday night."

He never asked me to a meeting again. But Buber and Hasidism! It was all I heard from him. He typed over his favorite Hasidic story and thumbtacked it to the wall over his desk.

"Well, what do you think?" he demanded, when I had read it through twice.

"It's very interesting. Very nicely written. Nice and concise."

"But a lot of crap as far as you're concerned."

"No, I wouldn't go so far as to say that."

"Then what?" he insisted.

"Well, for one thing, you have to believe that prayer works."

"And you don't."

"To tell you the truth, I never think about it. I haven't prayed since I was a kid."

"What happened?"

"I grew up."

He grinned—"touché"—and lit a cigarette, blowing the smoke from his nose, while I read the story once again. I can't remember the exact words. It was the one explaining the biblical injunction against using a metal tool to shape a sacrificial altar. The point being that God more often responds to a rough heaping up of stones; that is to say, a spontaneous, unpremeditated cry from the heart.

"Did you ever study any Hebrew?" he asked me, sitting down on the bed.

"Some. For my Bar Mitzvah, when I was a kid."

"Can you read that?" He pointed to the Yale motto emblazoned on the back of the rocking chair he had bought when he was an undergraduate, and still kept in his room.

"No. Let me see. How do you like that? I don't think I ever noticed it was in Hebrew before."

"It was once a required language here, you know."

"I had no idea."

"Oh yes. And not just for divinity students, either, but for all the undergraduates, along with Latin and Greek. My great-great-grandfather learned his Hebrew at Yale."

"What did he do with it after he graduated?"

"Prayed in it."

"A Presbyterian?"

"You'd be surprised. He came from Vermont, and at that time, in New England, it wasn't that unusual."

"Well, if I could, I'd put in a good word for you myself."

"Yes"—he laughed—"it wouldn't do any harm."

And so it went, our whole final year, when we were rooming opposite each other, in Sterling, on the third floor. When spring vacation came, and I was packing to leave for New York, he wanted to know if my parents were going to celebrate the Passover the following week.

"No. Well, yes, in a way," I said. "We generally have a family get-together, but no religious service or anything like that. A big dinner."

"And your mother makes gefüllte fish."

"No, Pearl."

"Who's that?"

"The colored maid."

He burst out laughing, and then looked at his watch. "What time does your train leave?"

"Six-fifteen."

"You've got a couple of hours. Why don't you come over to Payne Whitney with me and take a swim. The exercise will do you good."

He was beginning to put on a little weight around his middle, and generally worked out once or twice a week to keep in shape. While I took a quick dip and dried off, he swam his usual twenty laps, and came up the ladder at the deep end of the pool, gasping for breath.

"I want to apologize," he said, jumping up and down on one foot to get the water out of his ears.

"For what?"

"For asking so many questions."

"Forget it."

We got dressed and strolled back to the dorm. "It's hard for me to explain," he went on, as I opened the door to my room. "It's just that ever since I was a kid, He's been very real to me as a Jew. I mean as an actual Jew who once lived. Have you ever read the *Spiritual Exercises of Ignatius Loyola?*"

"No."

"It's not important." He sat down while I finished packing. "When I was ten or twelve, there was only one Jewish family living in town, or one religious Jewish family. An old man who owned a clothing store, who wore a long black beard, and what-do-you-call-them? You know what I mean. The long curls. . . ."

"Payis."

"Yes, that's the word. The curls tucked behind the ears. I can't even remember his name. He and his wife lived in one of the red-brick houses near the railroad station, on Old Steamboat Road. They never had any kids." He paused for a moment, thinking. "Goldfarb! That was his name! 'A Jew, a real live Jew' was all I could think whenever I saw him. Not so much like Him, perhaps, but maybe Joseph. Yes, why not? It was entirely possible that Joseph looked something like that when he was an old man, with that black skullcap and scraggly beard. And from there, of course, almost without thinking, it was easier to picture the Son when I prayed. Younger, of course, much younger, and maybe taller and thinner, but with the same bushy eyebrows, and the three furrows on His forehead that made a V when He frowned. You know the way kids are. The kind of imagination they have. And it was much easier for me to pray with a picture in my mind. I was right. Christ was a man, as well as God. That's the mystery of the thing."

I was puzzled why he hadn't gone to Divinity School to begin with, and become a pro.

"That's exactly why," he explained one afternoon, about a month before graduation, when I had gone into his room to borrow some of his class notes.

"I don't understand."

"A professional!" He grimaced. "How can anyone presume to be able to inspire a bunch of people at, say, ten o'clock sharp every Sunday morning for the rest of your life? And particularly if you're getting paid to do it? Hell, no. I'd rather be a lawyer who prays only when the spirit moves him. What was it you wanted?"

"Yesterday's class notes on *Bennedict versus Ratner.*"

"I haven't finished typing them up."

I'm almost finished with his story. He and Nina met after graduation, at a party that following October given by Bill's parents to celebrate his passing the Connecticut Bar exams. Her father is a judge. She was a Sarah Lawrence graduate, a psych major, who had been brought up as a Congregationalist. The first time that we were introduced, she told me that the only interest she had in religion was in getting Bill to walk down the aisle of a church. He laughed, and gave her a kiss on the mouth. This was after they had been going steady for a couple of months. They came down to New York on a Saturday night, just before Christmas, to go to the theater, and I met them for drinks at the old Sherry-Netherland bar.

"You two ought to get along very well," he said, waving at the waiter for another round.

"I can see it," I told him.

"He's crazy, of course," Nina said to me. "Stark raving mad."

"Of course." I nodded.

"He isn't, though," she added after a pause, with an exaggerated scowl. "That's the problem. He's completely sane. It's very disconcerting. According to the best authorities, a religious maniac ought to have an absolutely rampant Oedipus complex, a desperate need to placate the father. But he doesn't. Not a sign of it. I was absolutely brilliant in abnormal psychology, and I ought to know."

Bill laughed again. The waiter put down three more bourbon-and-waters. "Of course," she continued, "I'll grant you that I'm not exactly an objective judge of his condition." Bill put his hand on her arm.

"Merry Christmas," he said, leaning across the table, and kissing her cheek. "Merry Christmas, Milt."

"Merry Christmas."

The coming June, they were married at the New Canaan Congregational Church. For the next two years, Bill and I kept in touch by mail. I've saved all of his letters. The sprawling handwriting and huge margins on the left side of the page remind me of his class notes.

". . . It's lovely," he wrote, just after his father had bought them a home in Greenwich, on Old Bedford Road. "A converted ice-house, on four and a half acres of land, with a pond and an apple orchard. Nina makes sour applesauce. Milt, I never would have believed it was possible to be so happy. It's a little scary, to tell you the truth. I wonder why? I must ask Nina what Freud would say about that. Right now, she's washing her hair. Tomorrow is Sunday, but I shall sleep late and miss church. No matter. I pray at home. At night, particularly, when she's asleep. She sleeps on her back, with her hands above her head, the fists clenched. Last night, I woke up, and looked at her, and thought, 'God above, what more can a man want? Just let it go on and on, and when it comes time for it to end, let me be the first one to go. Take me. . . .'"

Etc., etc., dated August 10, 1961. Eleven months later, he was dead.

VICTORY:

A JOURNAL

27 July 1965

Beginning tonight, the kibbutz will be on special alert. In addition to the two men who stand watch every night until dawn, twelve more will take three-hour shifts. According to Shlomo Wolfe, this is the usual precaution against Syrian infiltrators when there's no moon.

Through his binoculars, I can see the grove of cypress trees that marks the frontier, less than two kilometers away. Behind it is OP One, the United Nations Observation Post, painted blue, and just beyond that, on the slope of the hill dotted with pine trees and scrub brush, is OP Alpha, the white UN hut in Syria. It's only when the sun flashes for a moment on a window, or a cloud of red dust is raised by a truck or a bus, that one is aware of the towns on the heights. And even then, at this distance, the glasses reveal very little: a cluster of whitewashed houses or a wisp of smoke. The army camps, with their artillery emplacements, are completely indistinguishable among the enormous black basalt rocks. Only Tel Azazyiat, on the summit of a small hill, six kilometers away, is clearly visible: a low stone building, with a flat roof, from which 120-mm cannon fire has for years been intermittently directed against Israeli settlements all along this part of the frontier.

"Accurate, too," says Wolfe in English.

He ought to know. Born in Safed, about thirty kilometers south-west of here, he has been a soldier since the age of twenty-one, when he fought in the 1948 War of Independence, and he still retains the rank equivalent of lieutenant in the Israeli army's active reserve.

"I'm on tonight," he tells me, as we walk back to his room across the parched lawn. "From eight to twelve. Come along if you like."

"I'd like to very much."

"Good. Can you handle a Mauser?"

"I don't know. I've never tried."

"It's simple. Come on and I'll show you."

His room is stifling. One of his children has left the screen door ajar, admitting a swarm of flies that light on my arms and legs to suck at the drops of sweat. I sit on the wrought-iron chair—one of the pair that he has made himself in the kibbutz machine shop in his spare time—while he rummages through the closet to get the automatic he keeps in a canvas holster, wrapped in a webbed belt, under a pile of shirts on the top shelf.

"Here we are."

He hands me the blunt gun, with its curious receiver, shaped like a fin, that forms the trigger guard and extends forward to an inch from the muzzle.

"How do you load it?" I ask.

"Just shove the magazine in the butt and pull back the slide."

"Is this the safety?"

"That's it. Right on the slide. Flip it with your thumb. That's the way. Give it here for a moment."

He inserts the magazine, unloads it again, and then slowly dismounts it while I watch.

"It's easy. First you cock the hammer, then press the slide catch. Here. Push the slide forward, like this, as far as it will go, and move it back and up. There, you see? The slide and the barrel come off together. Then you push the barrel forward against the spring, lift up the breech, and take the whole thing out of the slide. It's as simple as that."

"Now what?"

"Now you have to put it back together," he says. With his tongue rolled up between his lips, he resembles a child absorbed in a game. He's happy. Not because it's a gun, but because it's a complicated piece of machinery that fascinates him. I've seen the same expression on his face while he obsessively tinkers with some component of the kibbutz's electric generator, of which he's in charge, or the motor of my rented car. Handling any machine, his thick fingers, with their wide, cracked nails, seem to have a nervous intelligence of their own.

"I'll leave it in the closet," he says. "You can pick it up after dinner."

If the impending alert has upset the routine of the kibbutz, Marilyn and I are not aware of it. We have been here now for almost a week, and the day drags on, indistinguishable from all the others, wrapped in a luminous haze of light and heat.

4 P.M.

As usual, Shlomo and his wife, Aliza, are waiting for us on the lawn, along with their ten-year-old son, Adi, who has his father's pinched nose and his mother's beautiful dark eyes, with their black, curling lashes. He greets us in his preposterous gravel voice, then dashes off to join a bunch of boys his age kicking a soccer ball around with their bare feet.

It's the time of day when adult members of the settlement have finished work, and their children spend a few hours with them before going off to have supper in separate quarters of their own. A shout. The ball has been kicked into the trench that runs behind the infants' house, connecting it with the concrete command bunker to the right.

"What do you do with the kids?" my wife asks Shlomo.

"What do you mean?"

"When there's an emergency, like tonight?"

"Nothing."

"Don't they sleep in the shelters?"

"Not unless there's a danger of shelling."

He yawns, lying back with his hands behind his head. The ball has been retrieved by his son, who scrambles out of the trench and shouts something to the others that makes Shlomo grin. Aliza shakes her head in annoyance.

"What's he say?" Marilyn asks.

"Hara, Arabic for crap."

The kids continue to play, while in front of their stucco bungalows their parents relax. A long day's work, beginning at five in the morning, has exhausted them, and their faces show it. The men are sunburned and healthy-looking from working in the open. Without makeup, even lipstick, the women are pale, but flushed at the same time, with blotches of color on their cheeks, from the heat that has dried out their skin and given them premature wrinkles around the eyes and at the corners of their mouths.

Aliza has prepared coffee. "Where's your sister?" she asks Adi, who wanders over for a piece of fruitcake she offers him from a tin.

"At Sarele's, doing homework."

"Go and ask them if they want some cake."

"They'd say no."

"How do you know?"

"They're on a diet."

"It's true," says Aliza, in English. "I forgot. At thirteen, can you imagine? Fads. Last week it was—I forget what."

In less than an hour now, it will be dark. The dazzling sunlight, as yellow as the yolk of an egg, has already begun to shift and fade, turning the Syrian mountains a faint lilac.

Rye bread, cucumbers, carrots, white cheese, a choice of one hard- or soft-boiled egg, and a little dish of sardines, washed down by a cup or two of tepid tea: supper in the communal dining hall is always the same. By seven-thirty, the huge place is jammed, resounding with voices and the clatter of silverware and Bakelite plates. On our way out, Shlomo pauses by the door to talk with Rafi, who has recently replaced him as military commander of the kibbutz. An order from Israeli GHQ, Northern Area Command, has just been received on the phone: Our defenses will be reinforced by a contingent of special Border Police, who will camp in the field next to the new apple orchard.

Outside, a cool breeze has sprung up, swaying the tops of the poplar trees against a cloudless, blue-black sky, shining with innumerable stars. The mercury-vapor lamps, strung on poles along the flagstone paths between the trenches, cast a white light, tinged with purple and green, on the chatting couples drifting up the hill toward the children's houses to put their kids to bed.

The loaded automatic thumps against my thigh. With an Uzi slung over one shoulder, the muzzle pointing down, Wolfe leads the way behind the bungalows. We are in a pine grove planted as cover.

The trick, he explains in a whisper, is to make your rounds irregularly. Go back on yourself, wait awhile, and then move again, in the opposite direction, so that any possible infiltrator can't fix your arrival at any given spot.

We plunge on. Now and then, diffused light from one of the shaded windows of the rooms reaches us through the trees. Confused by the shadows, I stumble, and the branches lash at my face. Wolfe walks erect, his left forearm raised before him and sweeping back and forth like the windshield wiper of a car. He moves silently on the balls of his feet over the dry pine needles and twigs. Then he stops, kneels down on one knee, and raises his Uzi.

"What's the matter?"

"Shhh . . ."

We have reached the edge of a field. At first I can hear only the monotonous, rhythmical drone of the crickets and the faint rustle of the breeze in the thistles and camel thorns dried out by the sun. Then I throw myself down on my stomach beside him.

"What is it?" I whisper. "A truck?"

"No, listen," he tells me, a finger to his lips. The noise again, but louder, and in the distance, perhaps two hundred yards away, a moving red light that winks out and then reappears.

"That sounds like a truck shifting gears."

"No. It's a command car." Wolfe raises his voice. "Our Border Police."

We wait until the sound of the engine dies away and the red light disappears, engulfed by the darkness that has effaced the boundary between the earth and the sky. The mountains have vanished, leaving hundreds of flickering lights in the Syrian villages mysteriously suspended in space.

"There, you can see the lights in Azazyiat," says Wolfe. "And further up, Zaoura, one of their very heavily fortified villages. It's actually settled by their army. Conscripts and their families. Now look down, and to the left, straight ahead."

"It looks like a campfire."

"That's it. That's in Nuchele, right across the border. About a year ago, fifteen of their cows wandered into our pasture."

"What happened?"

"A big discussion in our general meeting. All very ideological. About our duties as socialists to the oppressed Arab masses." His

voice is filled with amused contempt. "On the other hand, returning the cows meant that somebody would have to cross the border
and take a chance of being shot on sight, or worse."

"What did you do?"

"Put it to a vote. It was decided to give the cows to our police,
who impounded them. But sure enough, two days later, one of
their old women shows up waving a white flag. A rag tied to a
stick." He laughs through his nose. "They would send an old
woman. She was scared to death, shaking like a leaf; a little dried-
up old hag, without a tooth in her mouth and blind in one eye. Rafi
and I spoke with her. My Arabic is pretty good. When we told her
we'd given the cows away, she thanked us politely and went back.
I thought that was that, but I was wrong."

"Why? What happened then?"

"That night, they made a raid. Took us completely by surprise.
Set fire to the haystack, first, near the silo, to attract our attention,
and in the confusion made off with fifteen of our best milkers."
Another laugh. "Fair is fair."

We pass the dining hall and quietly circle left, to the west,
behind the children's houses, where the mercury-vapor lamps cast
our gigantic shadows across the dirt road, rutted by tractor treads,
that leads to the orchard. All around us, a faint mist is rising from
the earth. When we leap over a trench, my left hand brushes a lilac
bush and comes away soaked with cold dew.

10 P.M.

Another quick cup of coffee in the Wolfes' room, where
Aliza and Marilyn have been passing the time reading old copies
of *National Geographic,* to which Shlomo subscribes.

"Everything okay?" Aliza asks.

Her husband nods.

"Actually, you never get used to it," she says. "Or I should say,
I never have."

She speaks English perfectly, with the remnant of a British
public school accent.

"A week or so ago," she continues, "infiltrators threw hand
grenades into a chemical tank at Amatzia, near Lachish. That's
down south. Luckily no one was hurt. But the next time . . ."

She offers me a cheap Israeli cigarette. The dry, loosely packed tobacco flares up and then goes out when I neglect to immediately take another drag, leaving a bitter taste in my mouth.

Shlomo and I go on with our rounds, down past the chicken coops, the cowshed, the silo, and the blockhouse that contains the electric generator. He goes inside for a moment to check the machinery. The throb of the engine reverberates in the air.

"In those circumstances, ideology is useless. Worse. Naive," he resumes, when we stop off at the dining hall for a drink from the water cooler near the door. "The Arabs hate us so much it's hard to believe. I know. I've seen the bodies of our men who've fallen into their hands. We're infidels to them. Foreigners and invaders."

I wait for him to continue, but he silently fingers the loaded magazine stuck in his belt. He and his wife helped found this kibbutz, and have lived here, according to its strict socialist principles, for almost seventeen years.

On the path are four border policemen wearing green berets and armed with Uzis and Belgian FNs. They are chatting with two other kibbutz members on night watch: Seymour and "The Chink," a short, fat Russian from Shanghai, who has the sleek, black hair of an Oriental and puffy eyes. Shlomo grimaces.

"We had the same type in our outfit during the war," says Shlomo. "Useful."

"For what?" I ask.

"To do the dirty work."

He describes a young sabra under his command during the crucial battle for Lod, on the road to Tel Aviv, during the summer of 1948. "Tall, thin, sandy hair. A born killer, who loved it.

"We were ordered to attack Lod to remove the threat to Tel Aviv from the south. It was between the first and second truce called by the UN. A complicated maneuver. A commando battalion, with an armored car, attacked first, then our brigade, from the southeast. We had a six-pounder with us and a few shells. The enemy resistance was strong. The Arab Leigon and armed Arab civilians and militia fought like hell. The commandos pulled out, but we captured the southeastern outskirts at night and managed to break into the center of town.

"It's very old, with an old church, the church of Saint George, and a mosque right next door, off the main street. We had word that another truce was coming, and we were ordered not to touch any of the Christian or Muslim holy places. The UN would send in inspectors, and we had to think of world opinion.

"There we were, in the dark, with a mass of armed Arabs who outnumbered us maybe three to one, or more, all hiding inside their houses, behind shuttered windows, or in that damn mosque. Officially they had surrendered, but we knew they were just waiting for the Arab Legion to counterattack. So we stayed up all night and sweated it out. It was too quiet. Not a sound. Eli, the kid with the sandy hair, comes up to me smelling of cologne. He's found a gallon of the stuff in an abandoned Arab shop and poured it over his head.

" 'Wolfe,' he says, 'I don't like it.'

"At dawn, the very first light, the Arabs opened up. Rifle and machine-gun fire from everywhere. Five of my men went down. The Arabs yelled, 'Itbach el Yehud!' 'Kill the Jews.'

"More shots, and hand grenades, tossed from the door of that mosque. They exploded right in front of me, killing three more of my men. Two more grenades. When the smoke cleared, I got up from the street and ran back to the six-pounder. The crew had already loaded it.

" 'The mosque?' they wanted to know.

" 'The mosque,' I said. 'Fire.'

"It was point-blank range. We sent two shells through the door, and after the explosions there was silence. For maybe a minute. Then, all at once, the Arabs poured out of their houses with their hands up and threw their weapons on the ground. The uprising was crushed. We had the whole town. We started sending the prisoners back to their own lines, with a safe-conduct.

"Then I looked inside the mosque. The whitewashed walls were splashed with blood. In that small space, with thick walls, the shells had killed everybody. Men, women, and children. Maybe twenty-five people. What would the UN say to that? I thought to myself, I'd better dump the bodies on the outskirts of town, then wash the walls of the mosque. I gave the orders.

"We grabbed eight Arab men who had just surrendered, made them carry out the bodies in blankets, and then washed the place clean. But then I thought: the eight. What about them? They're witnesses. And they'd talk, too, I knew it. They'd tell the UN—everyone—that Jews massacred a bunch of Arabs in a mosque.

" 'Well? Who volunteers?' I asked my men.

"Nobody moved. Not a muscle. They all knew what I meant, but nobody said a word.

" 'It's O.K., lieutenant,' says Eli. 'I'm your man.'

"There was no expression on his face. Absolutely nothing. It was sweaty and filthy. He picked up his Bren gun.

" 'All right,' I told him. 'Do it on the edge of town. But fast.'

" 'Don't worry about a thing. Yellah! Let's go,' he says in Arabic.

"They shuffled off. I heard the shots. Lod was ours. Tel Aviv was saved. I did what was necessary. I'd do it again."

> 31 May 1967
> Dear Hugh and Marilyn,
>
> What fun to know that Switzerland is nice, in spite of the bad weather. Maybe it'll clear up in Geneva.
>
> I'm sitting quietly in the room listening to a concert on the radio —Brahms's Fourth. Everything has happened so suddenly that we're still in a state of shock. One by one, the men have disappeared, because they have been called up, and the kibbutz has been left almost alone to us women. Of course we too are on the front and have to prepare for war, as incredible as it seems. God help us, I can see no other way out, and the thought is almost unbearable. I must say, though, that we're not despondent and the mood is generally good. We're so busy that we really have no time to think.
>
> To add to it all, Shlomo had an unexpected appendix attack on Friday and was in the hospital for a few days. They will eventually have to take it out. He came home today feeling reasonably well, but I've hardly seen him. To be honest, I didn't know whether to be pleased or not. What, after all is safer—to have a comparatively minor operation or every night to be laying mines under Syrian guns?
>
> The children—all the children are wonderful and seem to understand that they must behave themselves.
>
> How wonderful it would be if you could come. Maybe, please God, this will prove another false alarm and you can come just for fun.
>
> Much love to you both from everyone,
>
> As ever,
>
> Aliza

9 June 1967

Is the dog dead? A small, black, shaggy mutt, with yellow eyes, lies in the corner of the restaurant, in front of the pickle barrel, impervious to the Israeli artillery barrage. His ears twitch, but only when I offer him a French-fried potato does he rise to his stumpy legs. The fourteen-year-old waitress stands in the doorway of the restaurant watching another helicopter bring down the dead and wounded from the slopes of the Syrian mountains to the hospital here in Safed.

I can see nothing outside. The barrage, obviously raking the Syrian emplacements, seems to double in intensity, but the guns are completely concealed. Their firing echoes and re-echoes in the narrow street, between the low stone houses. An old Rumanian couple—sit on folding chairs in the sun. We are on the highest plateau in the country; the air is cool.

More and more artillery. I run to the main street, Jerusalem Road, where I have parked my car. It's a little red Volkswagen, rented from Hertz last night, when I arrived in the country in the first plane out from Zurich. I learned this morning in Tel Aviv that Israeli settlements along the Syrian frontier have been under intensive artillery bombardment since Monday, and early this morning Israeli troops and tanks began the assault of the Syrian heights. All day long I have crawled behind military convoys going north: open trucks and buses, ordinary civilian buses filled with troops, husge 300-hp Mack tank carriers transporting British Centurions or Super-Shermans—American Sherman tanks refitted by the Israelis with thicker armor, diesel engines, and 100-mm guns.

Six, eight, ten more rounds. "One fifty-fives," says the bored MP in the middle of the street. "The direct road north from here to Kiriat Shemona is closed to all civilian traffic."

"But I've been stuck here for almost three hours."

"Listen to me. Find a decent hotel, the Herzia, for example, take a shower, have supper, and go to bed early. By tomorrow morning, the chances are you'll be able to get through."

He's a sergeant, with a splendid black mustache, who speaks English perfectly, although with a slight, undefinable European accent.

"What about the long route?" I ask him.

"What do you mean?"

I've been studying a tourist map. "Suppose I go back to Meron, north to the Lebanese frontier road, then head east until I connect with the main road north again?"

"Along the Lebanese frontier?"

"Why not? There's been no fighting, has there?"

"Be careful," he yells, as I start the car.

"I will."

"The road is lousy. You'll have to hurry if you want to make Kiriat Shemona before dark."

The frontier road is a single, unpaved track strewn with stones. I drive as fast as I can. The sun is setting. I glance down the steep slopes to my left at a Lebanese village: stone houses with red-tile roofs. A huge carob tree, to which a cow is tethered, spreads its lengthening shade. Not a glimpse of a human being.

Explosion after explosion on the slopes up ahead. The car rattles over the stones. At first I can hear nothing. Orange and white flashes; black smoke. Then a faint booming.

I see the reflection of the setting sun on a plane as it banks to the east.

7 P.M.

Kiriat Shemona is blacked out. The road is lined with troop carriers, half-tracks, Super-Shermans, and Centurions heading for the front. At the junction just north of town, a few kilometers from the kibbutz, the MP refuses to let me pass.

"Listen a minute," I tell him in Hebrew.

"Do you speak English?"

"Yes."

"Then fuck off."

He waves on a Centurion and a self-propelled French 105. I pull off the road, turn off my headlights, and wait in the dark. The MP has a flashlight with a red lens. He shines it in my eyes.

"You don't understand English?"

I drive back to the police station in Kiriat Shemona.

"It's no use trying to get through tonight," says the officer in charge. "The kibbutzim are still being shelled. Stay here. I'll take you to a hotel where you can get something to eat and some sleep. Believe me, it's the best idea."

Behind him, across the room, a Moroccan cop is thumbtacking a "wanted" poster to the bulletin board. The criminal's face is badly drawn. Except for his prominent ears, he could be almost anyone.

The hotel is about a kilometer away, on the other side of the main road. The windows have been painted blue. Inside, two flickering candles illuminate a few tables, chairs, and a refrigerated display case in which there are some bottles of milk and beer. The owner is an unshaven man, with white whiskers, who wears a yarmulka. Tonight is the beginning of the Sabbath. All he has for me to eat is the warmed-up half of a boiled chicken, cold mashed potatoes, and green beans.

"When they first came they were animals. But a few years in Eretz, a little education, and you'd be surprised."

The old man talks to me in Yiddish, which I can hardly understand, about the non-European immigrants in Kiriat Shemona.

"Have you got a beer?" I ask.

"One beer. Certainly."

The fatty, yellow skin of the chicken, with its pimply feather follicles, suddenly nauseates me.

"Never mind the beer," I tell him. "Where's my room?"

It's a cabin, sparse but immaculate, with two beds, a shower, and a clean towel hanging on the bathroom door. As soon as I'm alone, I go outside on the wet grass in my bare feet. The night is cold. The traffic on the road has ceased. Spread out to the east above me are the Syrian mountains. It's obvious that the Israelis have taken the slopes. A gigantic fire is raging far beyond the crest, blotting out the nearby stars. The fire grows larger, and for a moment it seems as if the sun were trying to rise in the middle of the night.

10 June 1967

"It was a miracle. No one on the kibbutz was even scratched," Aliza tells me. "Thirty boys were called up for the army, and we haven't heard from any of them yet, but the bunkers protected everyone here.

"It started last Monday, at exactly a quarter to ten. The small

hand siren went off. The trenches filled with people carrying kids
to their assigned bunkers. I went to mine. We'd been practicing
for three weeks, but this was the real thing and everyone knew it.
They all behaved beautifully.

"Then the shelling started. Sometimes there was a whistle and
a thud, sometimes just a thud. The earth shook."

"Eighty-two-millimeter mortars and one-twenty-millimeter
cannons," says Shlomo. "There were about forty hits within the
area of the kibbutz itself, but no major damage. Come on. I'll show
you."

At the silo, he collects a handful of razor-sharp metal fragments
in the red earth. "A mortar," he says. "Strictly anti-personnel.
That'll give you some idea of what it can do to a human being."

He points to the deep holes that pit a concrete wall of the
building.

"Have a look at this, in the field."

I'm wearing sandals. The thistles make it hard to walk.

"Just a little farther," he says. "Right here."

It looks to me like a large gopher hole, dug obliquely into the
ground. On his hands and knees, Shlomo reaches in with his right
arm up to the shoulder, and shakes his head. "I can't touch it. It's
buried too deep."

"What is it?" I ask him. "Why is the hole all burned like that?"

"It's a dud," he says. "A one-twenty-millimeter shell that didn't
go off. There are a couple more down in the orchard and one near
the chicken coop. I'll have to dig them up and defuse them."

He takes me through the new trenches that face the Syrian
frontier. At one of the forward salients, reinforced by sandbags
and covered with a sheet of corrugated iron, Shlomo's pal Amos
is working furiously over a machine gun.

"The damned thing is jammed again," he says. "I just stripped
it this morning."

Shlomo and I go back. In an open woodshed—on top of a pile
of bound bales of hay—a telescope has been set up. Gazing
through it at the steep slopes of the Syrian mountains, I can clearly
see two Israeli Centurion tanks with their hatches open and their
cannon pointing down. Greasy black smoke. The one on the right
is on fire.

"Was that the big fight last night?" I ask Shlomo.

"The breakthrough, on the plateau, to Quneitra. It's a fairly big city—their GHQ for the whole area. Apparently that did it. I've heard that they've accepted a cease-fire for six-thirty tonight."

Through the telescope, I can see three Centurions racing up the slopes. "Where's the fighting now?" I ask.

"We're mopping up everywhere."

"Are the Syrians any good?"

"Some run, and some fight like tigers. It took two hours of hand-to-hand fighting at Tel Azazyiat yesterday before they surrendered."

"He went out and mined the Syrian positions every night for three weeks before the war," Aliza tells me. "I knew what he was doing, but he refused to talk about it. You know how he is. When the doctors told him he could postpone his appendix operation, he couldn't leave the hospital fast enough to get back here and go to work.

"He got home about four A.M. I couldn't sleep a wink. I kept thinking about a boy I saw at Tel Hashomir hospital, where Seymour got his prosthesis. A mine had exploded in the boy's face. His jaw had been blown away; he had no tongue, no eyes. That could have happened to Shlomo. More iced coffee?"

"No thanks."

"Have you seen our new refrigerator?"

"It's lovely."

"The ice cubes are too small."

"Tell me more about the war."

"I only saw about ten minutes of it, early yesterday morning, during an all-clear, when we were allowed out of the shelters to watch our planes bombing the Syrian positions and our tanks attacking the fortifications.

"There are no roads up there, so they had unarmed bulldozers from the kibbutzim in the area make a path for them. When one got hit, they shoved it aside and brought up another to take its place. Then the siren went off, and we went down to the bunkers again.

"We were there from Monday until this morning, just before you came. There were enough all-clears to allow the children to go to the toilets in the trenches and get a breath of fresh air. One night Edith even had enough time to cook chickens in the oven. We had stocked up enough food and water to last us three months if necessary. But roast chicken! It was delicious.

"I was in charge of a bunker with eighteen adolescents and three babies from three weeks to four months old with their mothers. We all slept on twenty-one three-decker bunks, about a meter and a half long. We didn't sleep much. The mothers were terrified of rolling over and smothering their babies, and the older children wanted to go out and watch the fireworks. It was some job controlling them. The girls giggled a lot.

"I was never actually frightened—there was so much to do—until one night Seymour rang up from the command bunker and asked if we had a man and a shovel.

" 'Why?' I asked him

" 'I was just wondering,' he said.

"A few minutes later, during the shelling, one of the men arrived with a shovel. Then, all of a sudden, it occurred to me: He had been sent here in case a shell collapsed the entrance and we were buried alive. We would need a man to dig us out. I didn't panic, but my God, when the all-clear sounded, it was good to be out in the open air for a few minutes, under the stars."

Seymour drops by, thumping on his artificial right leg. Two summers ago, he drove his John Deere tractor over a Syrian mine —15 kilos of layered explosives, which the Israelis call a sandwich. Except for his missing right middle finger—he's forced to hold a cigarette between his thumb and forefinger—and a pronounced limp, he seems well.

When he leaves, Aliza tells me that he learned to use his prosthesis in almost half the time it usually takes.

"In spite of a horrible setback," she says. "One night, when he was still on crutches, he tripped on his way to the dining hall to see a film and fell right on his stump. It was black and blue—a massive internal hemorrhage which had to be drawn off in the hospital."

She returns with her kids Adi and Ruthie. In two years, Ruthie has become taller and more beautiful. Her face is thinner, dominated more than ever by her dark eyes. Proud of her figure, she wears brief shorts and a tight blouse with an embroidered collar.

Just twelve, not yet pubescent, Adi remains the image of his father, with his stocky build. They chatter away and laugh.

Aliza and Shlomo talk about the war, particularly the liberation of Jerusalem and the radio broadcast of the blowing of the shofar at the Wailing Wall.

"Lots of people cried," she says. "To tell you the truth, so did I."

"That's all this country needs!" says Shlomo. "A religious revival!"

The children go outside. "A couple of weeks ago, while he was studying the Bible for an exam, Adi asked me if I believed in God," says Aliza.

"What'd you tell him?" I ask.

" 'Sometimes.' I told him that sometimes, in spite of everything, I believe in something eternal and much greater than man."

"What'd he say to that?"

" 'Me too, Mama. So do I.' "

"It's six thirty-five," says Shlomo, glancing at his wristwatch. "The cease-fire's been on for five minutes."

We leave the room. The lights in all the bungalows have been turned on.

"Off! Turn off all the lights! Blackout!" Seymour calls out from down the path. "I just got a call."

We turn off the lights in the room, and Aliza checks the contents of a canvas bag she had in the bunker during the war: one long-sleeved shirt, a pair of heavy work shoes, a paper bag filled with a flashlight, a pad of paper, two pencils, matches, four candles, a comb, and a deck of playing cards.

Shlomo comes in. "Forget it," he tells her. "It was a false alarm."

"Are you sure?"

"Positive. Some idiot made a mistake. Let's go eat. Hugh can say hello to everybody."

Ten Israeli flags are flying outside the dining hall.

After dinner we remain where we are. Bottles of beer and sweet white wine are placed on all the tables. The room is crowded. Over thirty South African Jewish volunteers, all in their twenties, have been here since last Sunday. They came to replace the men who were called up.

Seymour's wife, Edith, is sitting with the saba, her father. He wears a black felt hat, with a round, stiff, wide brim, a long gray double-breasted coat, and knee-length white stockings: the costume of a Hasid. His beard has been carefully combed into two points, and he looks younger and healthier than I've ever seen him. As a matter of fact, it's the first time I've seen him in the dining hall at a public function.

Aliza has told me that he was perfectly calm in his bunker, reciting his morning prayers with his phylacteries, which he keeps in a ragged red-velvet bag. His daughter carefully stored separate dishes under his bunk, and a supply of tinned kosher meat. But he was perfectly content to live on dairy dishes—a little kosher sour cream, cheese, bread and butter.

Rafi stands up and makes a brief speech about the origins of the war from what army intelligence has told him. My Hebrew is rusty, and Edith must provide a running translation. She's so tired that she leans her head on her hands and speaks with her eyes closed.

Rafi catches my attention with two statements: one, that in the event of an early, concerted armored and infantry attack by the Syrians, the Galilee would have had to hold out on its own, without help from the army, for the first thirty-six hours; and two, that three weeks ago, two battalions of one thousand highly trained Egyptian commandos were sent into Jordan with instructions to split Israel in half. It was their jump-off signal, in code, radioed from Egypt and intercepted by Israeli intelligence, that prompted Israel to attack Egypt on June 5. Some of the commandos managed to infiltrate as far as two miles from Tel Aviv before they were captured; others are still at large.

A South African boy who has just entered the room lets the swinging door bang against a chair. Rama darts from beneath a table, quivering, with her ears back and her tail between her legs. Everyone laughs.

"She's a terrible coward," says Edith. "During the shelling, she lay in one of the bunkers quivering like that the whole time. She drank a little water but wouldn't eat anything."

"No wonder she looks so thin."

Amos, the new secretary of the kibbutz, stands up and asks for a moment of silence for those who have fallen for their country. When he raises his head, he pours himself a glass of beer and proposes a toast to peace.

Edith and I drink out of the same glass. "Don't cry," she tells me.

"Please don't cry. Everything's all right now. Take my hanky. Blow your nose."

Some of the South Africans turn on a phonograph and begin dancing a hora to "Hava Nagila." The kibbutz members leave to get some sleep.

"Look at the Syrian mountains," says Aliza. "No lights. Not a light anywhere up there for the first time in twenty years."

11 June 1967

We've been receiving messages from the boys in the army. Twenty-five are safe. Three have been wounded, and two are missing. As the day goes on, we get the details. One boy has been seriously wounded in the diaphragm by a bullet and has developed pneumonia. Another was been hit on the backside by shrapnel. The third took a bullet in the back, from a sniper, in the streets of the Old City.

I don't know any of the wounded or missing. Some have become members of the kibbutz in the last two years, and I can't remember the others.

At about three, Shlomo discovers that the army is holding twenty-six Syrian prisoners in the orchard. They were first taken to the police station in Kiriat Shemona, where a crowd of Jews from the Arab countries gathered and threatened to lynch them. Unable to handle the situation, the police asked the soldiers to bring them here.

We drive down to have a look. Two guards, armed with FNs, prevent us from getting too close. Hidden among the trees is a truck with a canvas roof; it's filled with men. One stands up. His hands are tied behind his back, and his eyes are blindfolded. He's wearing a white shirt.

Explosions and puffs of gray smoke on the slopes. It's Shlomo's guess that the army is blowing up the Syrian fortifications.

After dinner, I talk with Amnon, a member of the kibbutz who interrogated the prisoners this afternoon. He was born and raised in Syria and speaks Arabic fluently. He is the author of several children's books, and now he is the headmaster of all the kibbutz high schools in the area.

"They were all captured from army villages, like Zaoura, or the fortifications, like Tel Azazyiat. The peasants—that is, the ordinary soldiers, the conscripts—were completely passive, inert, hardly responsive to anything. They said they were illiterate. Two of them finally spoke up a little. We were about to feed them—bread, tea, eggs—when one started to moan, 'I won't eat eggs. Eggs make me sick to my stomach. You can't make me eat eggs.'

"Another claimed to have just gotten out of the hospital with a broken leg. He complained that if the doctors had kept the plaster on for a few more days, he wouldn't be here now.

"The officers, who were educated, were terrified we were going to shoot them. They said they had been given orders to spare no one and therefore expected the same treatment. One of them was a philosophy student from the University of Damascus. I asked him if he really believed all the propaganda on Radio Damascus about conquering Israel and exterminating the Jews. He thought a moment and then said, 'No, not really.' But he said he also never believed we'd be able to take the Heights.

"Then there was a sixth-grade schoolteacher from Zaoura, who claimed to be a civilian. He was in his middle twenties, but said he wasn't in the army because he was a teacher. He also said he remained behind when the fighting started to stay with his old parents. I asked him why they weren't evacuated, but he had no satisfactory explanation. He kept repeating he was worried because he didn't know what had happened to them.

"Then I asked him what he taught his pupils about Israel and the Israelis, and just like that, he answered, 'Probably similar to what you teach yours about us.'

"He was so quick and shrewd I had to laugh. I had the feeling he was lying. He was probably an officer in mufti. Maybe in Intelligence. I had the feeling they were all lying, to one degree or another, about something, in the hope that it might somehow help them. A cloud of lies, little ones, big ones, like ink squirted from a squid, to hide behind."

12 June 1967

A postcard has been tacked up in the dining hall from one of the wounded boys who is at Hadassah Hospital in Jerusalem. He sends greetings to all the members of the kibbutz but is sorry to say that he wasn't wounded in the bottom, as first reported, but a little higher. He's receiving wonderful care and thanks all those who sent him fruit and flowers and took the time to write him. He hopes to be able to write his next note himself. "Please find me an easy job in the secretariat's office," he says, "as I will now be useless in the cowshed."

"We called the hospital," Aliza says. "He has shrapnel in his neck, which damaged his spinal column. He can't move his hands at all, but the doctor assures us that he'll gradually regain use of them. There's still no word from any of the missing."

As school resumes tomorrow, Nat, the high school teacher, is busy in his room preparing the first lesson. I hardly recognize him. He has shaved off his mustache, revealing a long upper lip. As though an impediment has been corrected, or perhaps because I can see his lips move as he speaks, he seems to enunciate more clearly.

"It's very hard," he says. "I want to teach the kids about the consequences of the war and explain that all we want is to sign a peace treaty with the Arabs. If they don't, we'll continue to occupy Sinai, the west bank of the Jordan, and the Syrian heights, for our own protection. This means that we'll be regarded as conquerers by a million resentful Arabs. If they actively resist us and resort to terror, we'll have to retaliate.

"I've got to make them understand that we have a special responsibility to be as just and as merciful as possible. Our history demands it. All the anguish of the Diaspora. If we become oppressors now, after all of that, it would be a betrayal of everything that we are as Jews."

"What about Jerusalem?" I ask.

"What about it?"

"You didn't mention giving that up."

"No," he says, "and we never will. It's our historic capital. And then there's the Wall."

"What do you care about the Wall if you're not religious?"

"I've been thinking about that. When we captured it, I wept without knowing why. Why did the early Zionists, who were atheists, insist on returning here? Herzl, as you know, was offered Uganda as a Jewish national home, but the Sixth Zionist Congress refused to consider it. It has to be the land of Israel or nothing.

"It was as if they unconsciously assumed that a covenant between the Jews and God still existed. Deep down we feel the same way. It's depressing. You'd think that by now we'd be finished with Him once and for all."

He absent-mindedly raises his forefinger and strokes his clean-shaven upper lip.

"But is it possible to create a humane civilization without Him?" he says. "That's the question."

At nine-thirty in the evening, Amos comes into the dining hall, where eight of us have been talking, and announces, "Shimon has died in the hospital."

Everyone leaves without a word.

"What is it? What's happened?" I ask Edith. Although I understood the Hebrew sentence perfectly, for an instant I was incapable of assimilating its meaning. Shimon was the boy who was wounded in the diaphragm.

We go to the Wolfes' room where Shlomo turns on his stereo tape recorder—a resonant organ plays Bach's "Passacaglia and Fugue in C Minor."

"Do you hear the difference?" he asks me. "A beautiful tone. It's new. A Crossfield."

"I hadn't noticed."

"I traded in my Grundig and my old Leica and paid the difference in cash. It cleaned us out, but it's worth it, don't you think?"

"The tone is beautiful."

Edith and I sit together on the convertible sofa, Aliza in a chair to my right. We're joined by Seymour, Ruthie, and Nat, who has brought along a copy of *Maariv*, the evening newspaper. He opens it as soon as he sits down. Ruthie weeps.

"Shimon was the leader of her group," Edith explains. Her voice is hoarse from fatigue and smoking. "All the kids adored him."

Now the "Toccata, Adagio, and Fugue in C Major" resounds in the small room. "Make it lower," Aliza tells her husband. Instead, he takes two bottles of liquor down from the closet—a half gallon of Johnnie Walker Red, which I bought in the Zurich airport, and a pint of Wishniak, Israeli sweet cherry brandy. He pours out stiff shots of Scotch for Edith, Seymour, and himself and looks inquiringly at me. I shake my head.

Nat and Aliza sip a little brandy. Ruthie weeps again until her father whispers something in her ear. Then she laughs, blows her nose, and puts on a pair of dark glasses.

By ten-thirty, Shlomo, Aliza, and I have been left alone. A knock on the door. It's Esther, the nurse, breathless from excitement. She tells us that her husband has just returned home from the army and insists that we come over for a few minutes to say shalom.

The man, who obviously doesn't remember me, shakes my hand. His khaki shirt is torn at the right elbow. Filthy, unshaven, with a bad cold, he tells us that he was at Sharm el Sheikh, where the Egyptians deserted their bunkers, escaped into the desert, and then returned to surrender.

He coughs. Exhaustion makes him sounds as if he's drunk.

He says that he has it on good authority that the Egyptians on the other side of the Suez machine-gunned their own troops who had managed to straggle across the desert.

His wife, who has been unlacing his boots, raises her head. "But why?"

"To prevent them from spreading the truth? Who knows?"

13 June 1967

All the Israeli flags have been taken down in front of the dining hall, and inside, within a glass case opposite the door, is a photograph of Shimon, framed in black paper. It's an enlarged snapshot of him sitting cross-legged on the lawn in front of his room. Dark hair, dark eyes, and a mustache.

Except for the soldiers, who are camped near the orchard and are lounging everywhere, the kibbutz seems to have returned to normal. The men are back at their various jobs, and the women are particularly busy cleaning up and doing the laundry acumulated after five days in the bunkers.

Edith is helping out in the infants' house, preparing formulas for three babies. One of them is Shimon's four-month-old son.

Aliza comes in with a pile of clean infants' clothes she'd collected from one of the bunkers and begins sorting them out.

"Shlomo thinks that both Yaakov and Yehuda—the missing boys —are dead."

"Why?"

"He says we should have heard something from them by now. Yaakov's unit is now somewhere up in Syria, and Shlomo and Amos want to go up and check. I begged them not to. One of the officers told me after breakfast that it's absolutely forbidden unless you have a special pass. Three Israeli soldiers had their throats cut last night, and there's still sniping going on, and mines. Two boys were killed at dawn this morning. They went over a mine in a Jeep."

A khamsin today. Returning to the Wolfes' room at noon to take a nap, I run into Shlomo. He's in uniform—boots, leopard-skin camouflage pants, and a khaki shirt with the insignia of lieutenant on his shoulders. Over one arm he carries another khaki shirt and a pair of pants.

"Do you want to go up?" he asks me.

"Of course."

"Then put these on, and for God's sake, keep your mouth shut."

Amos is already in the covered Jeep next to the driver's seat with two Uzis beside him.

"You won't get any lunch," Aliza cries out.

Shlomo spreads red earth over the Jeep's hood and sprinkles it with a hose. The hot wind dries it immediately. Caked mud is the standard camouflage used on all the Israeli light vehicles I've seen on the way to the front.

I get into the back and brace my legs. Aliza waves. Her face is pale and contracted as though she were suffering from a violent headache. We drive away.

Although we were never friends, I suddenly have distinct memories of Yaakov from two years ago. For some reason, I picture him seated on the edge of a table in the dining hall, with one leg drawn up and his chin resting on his knees. He's squinting; was he myopic?

Beyond Kfar Szold we make a right. We climb the Syrian heights on a dirt track, raising cloud of red dust. We're almost vertical. I have to hang on to the back of Amos's seat with both hands. Shlomo stops; the dust settles.

Below us is a white shack—OP Alpha, the deserted UN Observation Post. A door has been left open. We're in Syria, or what was formerly Syria, surrounded by ripe wheat.

Off again. The dust clogs my nostrils. Another stop. To the left, just behind us, the burned-out hull of an Israeli half-truck that exploded. Ammunition cases, spent cartridges, and burned pieces of paper are scattered about, among the wheat, for a hundred yards.

Shlomo holds up a steel helmet perforated through the crown.

"Keep it as a souvenir," he tells me.

"No thanks."

He throws it away and drives on, higher, until he stops again.

"There you are. Straight down there. The back of Tel Azazyiat."

I can see only a concrete turret and the twisted branches of an olive tree.

"Can we get any closer?" I ask.

"Not on your life. You see those white tapes strung everywhere? Mines."

"How did they miss anything?" says Amos. "That's what I want to know. You can piss and hit anything in the whole valley from there."

As we go on, the dust hides my view, the Hula valley spread out behind us remains in my mind: the cultivated fields, the trees, buildings, and in the distance, reflecting the blue sky, artificial fish ponds.

Shlomo yells over the roaring motor, "The sight must have driven them crazy. No wonder they hate us!"

On the summit of the plateau, a paved road leads east into Quneitra. More wheat fields, as far as the eye can see, divided by low fences made from black volcanic rock.

"They had to sow and reap all of that by hand," says Shlomo.

"How can you tell?"

"The plots are too small. You can't get machinery in there."

An MP armed with an Uzi waves us to a halt. I slump down, with my arms crossed on my chest, my eyes closed.

"What'd he want?" I ask, when we're allowed to continue.

"He warned us against looting and wanted to see my special pass."

"What'd you tell him?"

"The truth. That we were trying to find out what happened to a friend."

A dead dog is lying to the side of the road. We slow down to avoid the carcass of a donkey with a swollen stomach. Two more dogs. The large brown one, on the right, has his mouth open. Its tongue lolls to one side. Another donkey, a colt, with a distended stomach. The brown dog gets up, stretches, with its forepaws extended, its rump in the air—it has a bushy tail—and trots off.

Quneitra, the deserted main street. Above the red-tile roofs of the stone buildings and shuttered shops, a white minaret. We pass a movie, advertising some Arabic film with a colored poster, half of which has been torn from the wall. Only a picture of a handsome, dark-haired man remains, holding out his left hand. A white rag on the end of a stick hangs from a balcony on which an Israeli soldier is seated, with his boots on the iron balustrade.

We park in front of the municipal police station, now Israeli army GHQ. The place has been bombed, and although the concrete façade is intact, all the windows have been blown out. Fragments of glass, rolls of toilet paper, Arab magazines litter the street.

"We're going inside to check," says Shlomo.

"O.K., I'll stay here."

"Don't speak English with anyone."

I climb down. At my feet is a large, framed photograph, covered by a cracked pane of glass, of a Syrian mother and her two sons. The woman is very old, dressed in black, with a black shawl over her head, and very beautiful. She has delicate features and large, clear eyes. The boys are in their early twenties. The one on the left is bare-headed and wears a double-breasted suit. His brother has a long kaffiah, with an argal, draped around his head. They gaze into the camera with much more diffidence than the old woman, whose look shows her love and pride. I glance around—no one is watching—smash the glass and the wooden frame, then pull out the picture.

"That's a souvenir worth keeping," says Shlomo.

He hands me a bottle of orange soda, which I gulp down without taking a breath.

"What about Yaakov? Any news?"

"His unit may be at Nafach or Sidiana. We have to go on."

We drive out of town to a junction; northeast, less than fifty miles away, is Damascus. The road is empty, guarded by two MPs.

We head south. The landscape is beginning to change. In the distance are the craters of extinct volcanoes. We turn off onto another dusty track.

"Nafach," says Shlomo.

We pull up under a grove of eucalyptus trees. Israeli soldiers are sleeping in the shade.

"Well?" I ask Shlomo, when he returns from the CP.

"Not here."

"Are you going to Fiq?" a fat soldier calls out.

"Maybe," Shlomo tells him.

The soldier climbs into the back with me, and under way again, we talk in English. He's an insurance agent in Tel Aviv and a tank-maintenance man in the reserve. He went up the Syrian slopes during the battle on Friday following the armor.

"It was my first combat," he says. "I didn't think I'd make it. I was sure I wouldn't make it."

Another camp. Tents in another grove of eucalyptus trees. Amos and Shlomo go to inquire about Yaakov's unit while the fat soldier and I wander around in the shade. We come to a pit filled with six prisoners dressed in ragged khaki uniforms. Their hands are tied behind their backs, and they're blindfolded with fringed kaffiahs. A Yemenite corporal stands over them with an Uzi. Darker than the Arabs, with coffee-colored skin, he wears a beard and earlocks. On the back of his head is a straw cowboy's hat.

We move closer. The prisoners lie on their sides. One was wounded in the right foot, which is bound in bloody rags. The man next to him suddenly raises his head to moan, "Yah Allah! Yah Allah!"

"If it was up to me, I'd shoot them all," says the fat soldier.

Back to the Jeep. "Sidiana, definitely," says Shlomo. In the wheat, a cow senses that human beings are passing in the road. She lumbers toward us, and I can see that her udders are full.

We wait fifteen minutes while four Israeli soldiers herd sixty Syrian women and children across the road. Some of the children are naked. All the women are barefoot. They wear identical shapeless black dresses and shawls, with strings of silver coins that dangle on their foreheads. A suckling infant wails. Its mother carries a folded mattress on her head. The women are loaded down with their possessions: pots and pans, brass trays and coffeepots, clay jugs, a glazed blue vase, bundles of clothing wrapped in blankets. They have obviously just been expelled from their village—mud huts set back two hundred yards or so, on our right.

"Where they taking them?" I ask Shlomo.

"To their own lines."

"But where are the men?"

"Interned."

"What about him?"

"Who?"

"The one in his undershorts."

Shlomo turns around. Behind us, less than ten yards away, a Syrian squats on his haunches, with his hands clasped on his head, guarded by an Israeli soldier. The Syrian shifts his weight, and the soldier raises the muzzle of his FN.

"Who's he?" I ask.

Shlomo says, "A sniper, maybe, or a terrorist."

With the muzzle now pressed against his right temple, the Syrian lifts his head and our eyes meet. He's in his mid-twenties, with broad shoulders and thick black tufts of hair under his arms. The Jeep lurches forward; we continue to look each other in the eye. Then he spits.

At Sidiana, Shlomo and Amos leap out of the Jeep and shake hands with a short officer. He clasps them both around the back of the neck, lowers his head to listen to their questions, and then replies for almost a minute. Shlomo nods.

"Yaakov's dead." Amos tells me. "He was napalmed by our own planes."

"Where? How did it happen?"

"At Jenin. He was part of an advance patrol that discovered some Jordanian Pattons and called an air strike down on them. Only they were too close and got it too." He spreads his hands. "His burned corpse was this long. About a meter."

Shlomo continues south toward the Sea of Galilee, rather than return to the kibbutz the way we came.

"We need time," he says. "We've got to think of the best way to tell his wife."

"The details?"

"No, of course not."

I yell, "Stop the Jeep!"

A barefoot Syrian boy of about sixteen dressed in a white shirt and blue pants, lies on his stomach in the center of the road.

"Is he asleep?" I ask.

Shlomo gets out and turns the boy over with his foot. The bloated face is yellow. There's a reddish blotch on the right cheek.

"He's too young to be a soldier," I say. "What's he doing here? Why didn't he run away?"

We drive past a burned-out Russian Jeep. The bodies of five soldiers are scattered around it. One lies directly in our path, and Shlomo swerves around him. His face is charred black, but his mouth is open. I can see his upper teeth. The fire has seared his left leg. Something—a buckle?—glitters.

Seven more bodies in the middle of the road are so bloated that their uniforms seem about to burst. The leather belt of one on the left has already snapped. His right hand is raised, the fingers widely spread. It resembles an inflated glove. The flesh is yellow.

A tremendous fart. I look around. The fat soldier is talking with Shlomo and Amos. Another fart as we drive away. I realize that it's from the asshole of one of the corpses.

It's eight o'clock by the time we return to the kibbutz. Shlomo and I walk up the path to his room past one of the children's houses.

"There she is," he whispers. "In the window."

"Who?"

"Yaakov's wife. No, don't look up. I don't want to talk to her now. She sees us. Keep going. Quick!"

Aliza asks, "What took you so long? I was worried sick."

"We went all the way down to the other side of the Sea of Galilee," I tell her. "And then north again, where we crossed the Jordan into Israel at the Benot Yaakov bridge."

I show her my loot: the photo of the Arab family.

"How could you?" she says. "That's horrible. Throw it away."

I tear the picture into shreds and toss it into the plastic garbage can in the toilet.

"But you must," Aliza is saying to Shlomo, when I go back into the room. "She's been waiting all day. She already knows he's dead. Five minutes after you left here, an officer from his unit came and told her. All you have to do is say a few kind words."

"It's not my responsibility. Amos is secretary of the kibbutz."

"Shlomo, you have to go and see her for a few minutes."

"I'm going to get cleaned up first."

"Are you hungry?" Aliza asks me.

"Starved."

"Take a shower, change your clothes, and I'll make you some eggs. How does that sound?"

"Wonderful."

We devour the fried eggs, white cheese, white bread, butter, and sliced tomatoes, and drink two glasses of iced coffee each. Shlomo finishes and goes out the door.

"Yaakov had a year-old son," Aliza says.

"I know. You told me."

"Did I? Yehuda is also dead. We got word this afternoon. He was killed in Jerusalem."

"Married?"

"Oh, no, he was very young."

Three-quarters of an hour later, Shlomo returns, saying nothing.

14 June 1967

Two more photos, framed by black paper, in the glass case in the dining hall. I recognize Yaakov immediately. The photo shows him without glasses. Yehuda is very young, thin and blond. His picture, taken from a distance, against a background of bushes, makes it hard for me to distinguish his features.

Aliza has told me that although the kibbutz will hold no religious services for the dead, it will go into mourning for two weeks. All public festivals, such as parties or movies, will be canceled.

With Amos and Shlomo in the Wolfes' room. Amos is looking through a Hebrew biblical atlas and has come upon a map of the Davidic and Solomaic kingdoms—the most extensive Jewish occupation of Palestine until now.

"Not bad," says Amos. "We held both sides of the Jordan and east as far as the Tigris and Euphrates as well."

"How long did it last?" Shlomo asks. "If the Arabs won't negotiate a peace treaty with us, we'll probably have to do it all over again in another five or ten years."

Left alone for a while, I come across Adi's copybook for his English lessons. He prints in a large, awkward hand on the lined paper. His last entry is dated yesterday.

The War

Last week we had a war. Israel had to fight Egypt, Jaardan, Iraq, and Syria. We won, but many soldiers are dead and many are wounded. The Arabs had many tanks, aerplanes, guns and bambs. But our men are better. Now we are happy and sad at the same time.

GOING UP

The truce with Syria went into effect at 6 P.M. At ten, I got a telegram from my uncle Mendel in Jerusalem. I borrowed a Bible from the kibbutz library and looked up the quote. It's from Psalm 121. "Behold, He who keepeth Israel shall neither slumber nor sleep."

Now that he had retired from the post office with a small pension, Mendel spent his time studying the Torah. He would have been completely happy if a widow with whom he had fallen in love had agreed to marry him. I met her only once, the month before, in Jerusalem, where she had inherited a kosher butcher shop on Ben Yehuda Street.

That was the day after Nasser had demanded that the UN withdraw its observers from Sinai and the Gaza Strip. I had gone to town to scrounge some ammunition from the army for an old German light machine gun we had. The army didn't have any. If the Syrians attacked, we would have to depend on a Hotchkiss and two Lewis .30-06's. One of the Lewis guns had a defective bolt. You had to be very careful with it. When the bolt slid forward, the damn thing went off by itself.

The widow remains in my memory standing next to the freshly skinned foreleg of a calf hanging from a hook on the ceiling.

"How old do you think she is?" he asked me on the way back to his flat.

"It's hard to say."

"Fifty-eight, can you believe it? She looks at least ten years younger, don't you think?"

"She's a handsome woman," I said, and he blushed.

"Did you notice her eyes?" he asked. "The same color as Anna's, may she rest in peace. That's what attracted me to her in the first place."

In his living room, a dog-eared volume of the Mishna lay open on his desk. He picked up a slim book, bound in black leather, next to the inkwell, then sat down and began reading.

His left hand covered the author's name, but I could see the title impressed in gold: *Tract on Ecstasy.*

"I promised Miriam I'd buy her a pair of sandals," I told him. "I'll be back in about an hour."

When I returned, he was stretched out on the horsehair sofa.

"I need her," he said. "I never dreamed I'd marry again, but what can I do? It's a fever in my blood."

"Then marry her."

"I would, if she'd have me. But Yoshe Dressner wants her too."

"Who's Yoshe Dressner?"

"A butcher who used to work for her husband and still helps out in the shop. And he's good. He knows the business. I can't deny it. I don't know anything about running a butcher shop." He sat up. "Still, she's a vigorous woman and needs a vigorous man, like me. Not an alter kocker like Dressner." He lapsed furiously into Yiddish. "An old fart of sixty-nine with arthritis."

He closed his eyes. His bearded face was suddenly ugly from exhaustion: yellowish and drained.

"Do you think there's going to be another war?" he asked me.

"I don't know. I hope not."

"What about the UN?"

"What good is the UN?"

"Yes," he said. "What can we expect from the goyim?"

"How about a bite to eat?" I asked him. "There must be a good kosher restaurant around here. What do you say? It's on me."

"No, I'm not hungry," he said. "But you go ahead."

It was getting dark. He switched on his gooseneck lamp, sat down, and, with his elbows on the desk, resumed reading. By the time I left to catch the 7 P.M. bus to the Galilee, his ears and the tip of his nose were bright red. It was as though the fever in his blood had abated for a while and then risen again.

He had been an *iluy,* a prodigy who was an accomplished Talmudic scholar at eight, and in his teens, the most brilliant student at his yeshiva in Warsaw. But at eighteen, when he married my mother's sister, Anna, he went to work for his father-in-law.

"He had a hardware store," he once told me. "A hole in the wall on Okopowa Street, right opposite the cemetery. We sold a little of everything. Nails, pots and pans, knives, coal, oil. You name it. We had to work ten, twelve hours a day just to make ends meet. My father-in-law, may he rest in peace, was getting old and needed my help, but he begged me to quit and go back to studying. 'You could become a famous rabbi,' he said. 'Rich and respected.' But that was the point. How could I do a thing like that? Make a profit from teaching what God has given freely to the Jews? God forbid! Anna understood; not a word of complaint from her, ever, may God rest her soul."

They couldn't have children, and when I was born, they loved me like their own. I was the reason they followed my parents to Palestine in 1932. My father had been a trade-union organizer for the Jewish Bund, but he realized there wasn't any future for Jews in Poland, became a Zionist, and emigrated. He worked for the Jewish Agency in Jerusalem and got Mendel a job selling stamps at the main post office on Jaffa Road. When my parents died within eight months of each other in 1946, I went to live with him and Anna in their two-room flat over a Hungarian restaurant on King George Street.

I was a socialist, like my father, and in the summer of 1949, when I joined the kibbutz, they raised no objections. Mendel said, "We'll come and visit you." Apart from attending my wedding in 1952, they never did.

Then, on the morning after the truce, at nine, he arrived, unannounced. He had bummed a lift on a truck carrying drums of machine oil as far as Afula, and another in an army Jeep to Kiriat Shemona. It was a Saturday—the first time I had known him to travel on the Sabbath.

"God forgive me," he said. "I couldn't help it. I had to see if you and Miriam were O.K."

"We're fine."

"God be praised."

Miriam chewed her lower lip. She had spent six days and nights in a shelter, under fire, and now had to help clean up the mess: hose down the concrete floor and walls, empty the chemical latrines, air the straw mattresses. Her eyes were red and swollen— she had been averaging three hours' sleep a night—but we would have to give up our bed to our guest and sleep on straw mattresses on the floor of our room.

What could we do? Mendel was sixty-six. The trip had almost finished him off. He had walked the two kilometers from Kiriat Shemona to the kibbutz lugging that cardboard suitcase in the broiling sun. He sat down wearily on the bed and carefully laid out the contents beside him: two pairs of underwear and socks, two shirts, a toothbrush, a plastic comb, and two knives, two forks, two spoons, and two plates wrapped in newspaper—one of each for meat and the other for dairy dishes—along with four cans of kosher beef stew, six jars of sour cream, phylacteries in a red-velvet bag, a silk prayer shawl, a prayer book, and a volume of the Mishna.

"What about your *Tract on Ecstasy*?" I asked him.

"What? Oh. I left that at home. It's very difficult, you see, and required enormous effort." He patted the volume of the Mishna with affection as if, like an old, beloved dog, it was incapable of surprising him and would never turn. "There are ecstasies and ecstasies," he said. "One must be very careful to distinguish between them."

He gazed with bleary eyes around the room and suddenly went on, "You might as well know it now. Hemda is going to marry Dressner on the twentieth of next month."

"I'm sorry to hear it," I told him.

"Yes," he said. "I'm sorry too." Then, rubbing his hands together, he smiled. "Nu, what are you waiting for? Aren't you going to show me around?"

"There's not much to see."

"Where were you during the fighting?"

"Manning the Hotchkiss in a trench next to the command bunker."

"You must have seen the whole battle for the Golan Heights."

"We were being shelled. I kept my head down most of the time. Once in a while, I took a peep through my binoculars."

"What was it like?"

"I can probably borrow our Jeep and take you up tomorrow if you like. That'll give you some idea."

"Wonderful."

"Now take a shower and get some rest," I told him.

"No," he insisted. "First show me around." So I took him on a fast tour of the kibbutz.

"Not one direct hit?" he asked.

"Not one."

He stared at the crater made by a 120-mm shell that had exploded on the road about ten meters from the garage where I worked.

"It's a miracle," he said.

The view, that night, of the Golan Heights left him speechless. It was something to which none of us, as yet, had become accustomed. The moon, in its first quarter, had just risen, and in its feeble light the mountains looked flat and dark. The lights of the Syrian fortifications on the slopes had been extinguished—for the first time in twenty years. We went back to our room, where Miriam was putting away some of my freshly laundered shirts.

"Did you get my telegram?" Mendel asked me.

"Yes."

"You don't pray, of course, but those particular words from the Psalm are part of the prayer that's recited before going to sleep," he said. "It's a good time to pray. The body is tired but the mind is extraordinarily clear. Do you know the feeling? Your thoughts echo, and sometimes it seems they carry very far. I don't think I ever prayed as hard as in the last month, even when Anna got sick."

"Coffee?" Miriam asked him.

"I forgot to bring a cup," he said. He was afraid that the few dishes we kept in our room for snacks might be contaminated by having been used for both meat and dairy.

"We only use the cups for coffee," I told him.

"Never soup?"

"Never."

"Then a cup of coffee, by all means," he said. "Thank you." But he stirred the sugar with his own spoon.

"It was wonderful being in Jerusalem last week," he went on.

"Did you know that our troops were ordered to attack the Old City through the Dung Gate but refused? Instead, they attacked through Saint Stephen's, in the Eastern Wall. They felt it was more dignified. And they were right; they were right. Did you ever imagine that you would live to see all Jerusalem in our hands again? I never did. It seems so strange and mysterious. Have you heard about the paratrooper crying at the Western Wall? Someone asked him why, and he said it was because he was from a kibbutz, and no one had ever taught him how to pray. It's a true story. I heard it from Hershel Glick, who was there. Do you remember Hershel Glick? He was there and swears it's true. It seems like a dream, doesn't it? It all has a hidden meaning you can't quite grasp."

He sipped his coffee. Miriam lit a cigarette, then said to me, "At least they're alive."

"Yes, that's something."

She was talking about three members of the kibbutz who had been wounded in action and were in the Hadassah Hospital in Jerusalem.

"Yora, you know, hasn't heard anything about Asher since Thursday morning," she said.

"I know."

Her eyes filled with tears.

"Who's Asher?" Mendel asked me.

"Asher Goldmann, one of our members. He's been reported missing in action at Sheikh Zuweid. Miriam and his wife, Yora, are good friends. They work together in the laundry.

Miriam said, "Asher's going to be twenty-one in November."

The next day, I lubricated our two GMCs in the garage. Miriam and Yora ironed shirts in the laundry, and twenty extra men were assigned to our cotton fields, which hadn't been weeded or irrigated in six days. It was touch and go whether we'd be able to save the crop. There was good news from Hadassah Hospital; none of the three had been seriously wounded. But there was still no news about Asher Goldmann.

Mendel spent the day in our room studying the Mishna. When I came back from work at four, I said, "Come on outside and get a breath of fresh air."

We sat on the lawn in the lengthening shadow of a poplar tree.

During supper, in the dining hall, Yora got a phone call from Goldmann's commander. He said Asher's half-track had gone over a mine at Sheikh Zuweid. The crew was dead. Their bodies were in the Beersheva military cemetery. If Yora wished, Asher would be exhumed and reburied on the kibbutz. She said, "I'd like that very much."

Yora hung up the phone, then asked me, "What happens when a half-track goes over a mine?"

"It blows up."

"Does it burn?"

"Sometimes."

"Was Asher burned alive?"

"No," I said. "He died instantly, in the explosion. You can be sure of it."

"How?"

Mendel said, "You must trust the Guardian of Israel."

The next morning was very hot. I overhauled the engine of one of our John Deere tractors in the garage, where the sun beat down on the corrugated metal roof.

At four, I got the use of our jeep for two hours. Miriam said it was too hot to take Mendel up, but he was adamant. She found him a straw hat with a wide brim and we took off.

I followed the path of the assault three days before: the rutted dirt track, marked by tank treads, behind Kfar Szold, which leads up the slope. It was so steep I had to stay in first and use four-wheel drive all the way. The wheels churned up a thick cloud of red dust that hung in the air around us.

Then I slowed down a little. Right below us was a white shack: OP Alpha, the abandoned UN Observation Post. The door had been left open. We were in Syria, or what had formerly been Syria.

"Go on," Mendel said. "Keep going. I'm choking to death." But after a few hundred meters, he grabbed my arm and shouted above the roar of the engine, "Ours?"

Just off the road, on the right, there was a Ford half-track—a troop carrier—which had taken a direct hit through the armored door next to the driver's seat, exploded, and burned. The barrel of the forward machine gun had buckled from the heat.

"Is it ours?" Mendel repeated.

"Yes."

"I can't breathe."

At the top of the plateau, I pulled up. The dust settled, the sun gleamed on some spent .50-caliber cartridges scattered ahead of us along the blistered asphalt road.

"Where does the road go?" Mendel asked.

"Straight to Damascus."

"We're in Syria?" He raised himself up, grasping the windshield, and gazed around him at the wheat fields strewn with black basalt boulders pitted like meteorites.

"At least they could have planted trees by the road," he said. "Something green. A little shade." And as he sat down again, the dry stalks of wheat rustled in a hot breeze. He held his nose and said, "Heavenly father! Where are the bodies?"

"In those fields."

"Why don't we bury them?"

"Do you want to go back?"

He shook his head, so I drove about three kilometers more on that vast plain while he held his nose and his beard fluttered in the wind. He looked younger. The dust had colored his beard a red-dish-brown and, like makeup, had covered the wrinkles on his forehead and at the corners of his eyes.

"Did you see that?" he called out. "The dog lying there? Its eyes were wide open."

I slowed down to avoid the swollen carcass of a gray donkey on its back. Its belly was enormous. Then there was another one, in a leather harness, and beside it, a bloated cow and her calf with a black and white face. Its belly had burst open; the entrails coiled on the road.

"The Torah forbids it," Mendel said. "It's forbidden to slaughter a cow and her calf on the same day."

There were two more dead cows, another donkey, and a reddish cow with a white face and markings on its flank. It looked like a pure-bred Hereford to me.

"Wait," said Mendel. "Stop."

Just ahead of us was a barefoot Syrian boy wearing a white shirt and faded blue pants. He was lying on his right side, his head resting on his outstretched right arm.

"Is he asleep?" Mendel asked.

"No."

"How can you be so sure? His eyes are closed. He looks asleep to me," he said, and before I could stop him, he bolted out of the Jeep. I went after him and, with my foot, turned the corpse on its back. It was getting ripe. The bloated face was very pale, but there was a reddish-blue blotch on the right cheek and another one on his throat.

"He wasn't a soldier," said Mendel. "He was too young for that. He can't be more than seventeen. What's he doing here? Why didn't he run away?"

"I have no idea."

"Was he married, do you think?"

"I doubt it. He was a peasant. They have to pay a bride-price, and it usually takes them years to save it up. Why do you ask?"

"I was just thinking. I was about the same age when I met Anna," he said, with his eyes fixed on the bloated face.

He crouched down. "Did you hear that? He's alive. He just belched."

"It's gas."

"Gas?"

"He's beginning to swell up."

"Are you sure?" he asked. "But what killed him? I don't see any blood."

"It's hard to say. Concussion, probably, from a shell. Yes, there's the crater over there. You see it? Near the road, where the wheat's been burned away?"

"A shell?" he repeated. "Theirs or ours?"

"What difference does it make?"

He looked up at me—his eyes were bloodshot from the dust— but said nothing.

And for half an hour after we got back to the kibbutz, he remained silent. We showered and changed our clothes. I fiddled with my short-wave and picked up the BBC World Service: a rebroadcast of a concert from the Albert Hall, in which it was hard to distinguish the applause and the Brahms from the crackling static. Mendel took down the borrowed Bible from the shelf above my bed and, seated in the wicker chair, read and reread a single page, mouthing the words under his breath.

Once, he said aloud, "It's a beautiful psalm."

"Which?"

"The hundred and twenty-first. And you know something? I believe it. I'm sixty-six years old, I've been around, but I believe it. He sees everything." He stroked his damp beard. "He never sleeps. One forgets. It wouldn't be so bad if I believed He was asleep."

THE THRONE OF GOOD

12 December 1946

Ari Rosenberg, who I now realize is a member of the Stern gang, has made an appeal to my professional conscience. A sixteen-year-old boy his organization has smuggled into the country from a British detention camp in Cyprus is ill.

"I think it's pneumonia," says Rosenberg.

"What're his symptoms?"

"You'd better have a look at him yourself," he tells me, and lowering his voice even though my office is empty, adds, "He's here in Tel Aviv. I've got him hidden in the cellar of an empty house on Hebron Street, near the Old Cemetery. He's been there three weeks."

"In this weather?"

"That's what worries me. He has a Primus stove, but we have had a hard time supplying him with enough fuel. The CID and the Haganah are on our necks right now, and we've got to be very careful about being followed. Unheated, that place is as cold and damp as a tomb. Will you have a look at him? He's had a bad time of it."

"What about your own doctors?"

"We can't be sure they're not being watched."

A gust of wind off the sea rattles my window. The glass is blurred by rain. And yet I can make out a woman huddled in the doorway across the street. She has gray hair. Is it possible that I'm under surveillance? Does the British Criminal Investigation Department employ middle-aged Jewish women as spies?

Rosenberg, who followed my glance, has also seen her but says nothing. He has already implicated me in his activities and knows that I know it.

"What's the boy's name?" I ask.

"What's the difference?"

"Suit yourself."

He repeats, "Will you come and see him?"

"All right."

"Good. Meet me exactly at midnight tonight on the corner of Tchernichovsky and Gan Meir."

"I'll be there."

"I appreciate it." And he adds, without any irony I can detect, "For old times' sake."

But at the door, he alters his tone. "During the Vilna Ghetto uprising, in the war, he took the name 'Zemsta.'"

"Zemsta?"

"Polish for 'revenge.'"

It's taken two hours—we doubled back twice on Rothschild Boulevard—for Rosenberg to lead me to the boy's hide-out: the cellar of a small abandoned house on Hebron Street. And now I wait alone for almost ten minutes in the back yard. The garden has gone to hell: a single pomegranate tree, above my head, sways in the wind. All its round, reddish fruits, bursting with juicy scarlet seeds, have long since dropped in the mud and rotted away.

The outside cellar door opens a crack, and Rosenberg whispers, "Come down."

He has a flashlight. The beam of light, flitting here and there, illuminates a small room: in one corner, an iron cot, a small table, and a Primus stove at the head of the bed, on the concrete floor. The air reeks of naphtha.

The boy is suffering from bronchorrhea, characterized by a slight fever at night—now a little over 38°C—diffuse rales, and a persistent cough that brings up a thin, purulent, yellow phlegm. As I have no antibiotics—there are none as yet available for civilians in the country—I prescribe aspirin, rest, and calcareose, 5 g, in chocolate-coated tablets to be taken three times a day.

He asks me in excellent Hebrew, "When will I be well enough to get out of here?"

"A couple of weeks."

"You can do better than that." Racked by coughing, he is unable to continue.

"Do you want the truth?" I whisper to Rosenberg at the head of the stairs. "That boy is going to get a lot worse unless you move him out of there immediately."

"It can't be done."

"Why not?"

"Our plans are set, and we can't take a chance of having him captured. Anyway, he's a volunteer. He accepts the risk."

He hands me the flashlight and draws a British service revolver from his side pocket.

"We have our orders."

"What kind of orders?"

"Turn off that light."

He opens the door, looks out, and says, "This way."

Stuffing the revolver back into the pocket of his mackintosh, he leads me across the yard, under the pomegranate tree. The mud sucks at our shoes. Hebron Street is deserted. Huge pools of water have gathered in the drainless street.

Rosenberg accompanies me home. Across Allenby Road, under a street lamp, a patrol of British paratroopers, whom our children have nicknamed "poppies" because of their red berets. Blue eyes, sandy hair, mottled, beardless cheeks: they are little more than children themselves, but each one has a Sten gun slung across his chest.

Rosenberg leads me around the corner. He is grinding his teeth together with such force that his jaw muscles bulge on the right side of his face, beside his ear. It's a habit he has retained from childhood. We grew up on the same block in Haifa, but in that dark mackintosh, with one hand thrust in a pocket gripping a gun, he has become unrecognizable to me. The bulging jaw belongs to someone else; none of our common childhood memories that might bind us together again is evoked: the smell of broiling kebab, mingled in the salty air with crude oil from the refineries; the one-legged Arab beggar, in black rags, sprawled on the sidewalk near the Town Hall, whom we passed every afternoon on our way home from school. Rosenberg, who was already proficient in idiomatic Arabic, would stop and chat with him. The beggar invariably refused our proffered coins.

"Why?" I once asked Rosenberg.

"Because I listen to what he has to say," he explained.

We were even in the same class at the Hebrew University, where he took a degree in Hebrew literature. I thought I knew everything about him, but realize I know nothing.

He has deliberately placed his pistol on the table between us. Has he killed anyone with it?

He drinks off his third brandy; his eyelids droop.

"Tell me about the boy," I ask.

He yawns. "There's not much to tell. He was born in Molodechno, where his father was a grain merchant, and his mother the only daughter of a cantor in Vilna. The father did pretty well. He started the kid in cheder at three and wanted him to go to a yeshiva and become a rabbi. The kid was bright enough, but restless. He skipped classes and roamed the fields with the local peasants. His father begged him to study, but it wasn't any use. The old man took a strap to him more than once.

"The whole family was deported to the Vilna Ghetto in May 1941. A month later, the parents were murdered in the pogrom in the Nowograd marketplace. The kid was saved because he was with his grandfather studying Talmud at the time.

"He ran away the next day, taking a bread knife and his father's prayer book. He joined the United Partisan Organization. The FPO. First he served as a courier, and then, the next spring, at the age of thirteen, he stabbed to death a Lithuanian policeman, a 'man-hunter' they used to call them, who helped the Germans round up Jews in the ghetto for extermination in Treblinka. As a result, the kid was posted to Itzik Beinisch's command on Staszuma Street, the building that was the first line of defense in the uprising against the Germans. They didn't stand a chance. Most of them were wiped out. A few hundred managed to escape to the forests outside the city or, like the kid, hide in the sewers until they were liberated by the Red Army in July of 1944."

"In the sewers?"

"In the sewers," Rosenberg repeats. "He spent almost eleven months in those sewers." He picks up his revolver and asks, "Do you know any songs of the Vilna partisans?"

"No."

"I'm translating some of them from Yiddish into Hebrew. We

want to bring out a Hebrew edition. But it's hard to preserve the idiom. Do you remember any Yiddish?"

"Some."

He recites:

> Sligt ergetz fartayet,
> Der feint vee a chayeh
> Der Mauser, er vacht in mine hant . . .

Then he translates:" 'The enemy' . . . 'harkens; a beast in the darkness; the Mauser wakes in my hand . . .' "

15 December 1946

For the past two days, I've been under surveillance, by that middle-aged woman lurking in the doorway across the street, and then, as I make my daily rounds, by a tall young man who wears a leather jacket. Today, making no effort to conceal himself, he followed me to the clinic (sponsored by the Zionist Federation of Labor) on Etzion Gever Street.

A few Arab women from Jaffa bring their children to be treated here for trachoma, boils, ringworm, and chronic dysentery. The boys amaze me. They lie naked and motionless on the sheet, under the overhead light, never uttering a sound, while I incise and then drain the boils that usually cover their buttocks and the backs of their thighs. The women, whom I hear through a thin partition, moan. This afternoon one of them fainted dead away. Observing the Arab custom, I had Miss Guinzburg, my nurse, remove her veil and bring her around with spirits of ammonia.

Finished at five, I walk, in the rain, to the café on Dizengoff, where I usually have a cup of Arab coffee and a brandy. Leather Jacket remains just outside. The rain has plastered his hair to his forehead and hangs in shining drops from the tip of his nose and his earlobes. As I am about to leave, a roving patrol of Royal Marines stops and carefully examines his papers. Apparently satisfied, the sergeant, who has a bristling mustache, shoos him away.

"Go on," the sergeant yells, "'op it!" and waits until Leather Jacket has boarded a bus on the corner.

Rosenberg, in his black mackintosh, is waiting for me outside the door of my flat.

"The kid's getting worse," he says. "Much worse. Will you come and have a look at him again?"

He insists on taking the usual precaution. We wander around the city for an hour and a half, until we reach the Old Cemetery and the cellar on Hebron Street. No one follows us. Apart from a solitary Arab policeman, armed with a British rifle, on Allenby Road, the flooded streets are empty. The Arab wears a *kulpack*, obligatory for native police. It's a kind of fez made from black lamb's wool. But it's much too big for him, and as he turns his head to watch us pass, it slips down to the bridge of his nose.

On the table in the cellar a flickering candle, stuck in its own grease, on an overturned glass, throws our enormous, leaping shadows on the whitewashed wall.

"It's freezing down here," I tell the boy. "Do you want to catch pneumonia? Why don't you use that Primus?"

"I ran out of fuel yesterday."

"I'll try and send him some tomorrow morning," Rosenberg says.

"The cold doesn't bother me," the boy says.

He is suddenly convulsed by a cough and he spits into a filthy handkerchief. The sputum now is grayish white and separated into an upper layer capped with frothy mucus and a thick sediment in which there are dirty yellow masses. He has developed putrid bronchitis.

"Well?" Rosenberg asks.

"You'd better get him to a hospital tonight."

"I can't."

"There's nothing I can do for him here."

"Don't you understand? He has forged ID papers, but the CID has a complete dossier on him. They know he's in the country. If they catch him, they'll cure him all right, but then what do you think will happen? He knows too much, but he won't talk. At least not under physical torture. But they're smart. They'll keep him in some cell in Acre."

The boy repeats, "In Acre? Underground?" He shakes his head. "No, I don't think I could take that. I've already been down here almost a month. I hear things."

"What kind of things?" I ask.

"A rattling chain and a growling dog. A dog at the end of a long chain tied to the doorknob, at the head of the stairs, outside."

"It's only your fever. It'll pass."

He says, "You think so? I'm not so sure. The SS in Vilna sometimes chained vicious dogs to the gratings on the streets to prevent us from coming up at night to scrounge around the city for a bite to eat."

"Did you ever try to escape through the sewers to the forests and join the partisans?"

"I was fated for other things. For a long time, I had a whatchamacallit—I don't know the word in Hebrew. You know, from a bad knock on the head."

"A concussion."

"Yes. I was on the second floor of our headquarters on Staszuma Street, stuffing a rag into a bottle of gasoline. The Germans were attacking. There was a bright flash. The ceiling fell down. The next thing I know was that Shmuel Epstein, one of Itzik's lieutenants, was carrying me on his back through the sewers. That's very vivid. My head ached something terrible, but I hung on, my arms wrapped around his neck, with all my strength. He had a pillowcase, a linen pillowcase stuffed with something, between his teeth. Once he forgot himself and opened his mouth to speak to me, and it dropped into the filth.

" 'What's in it?' I asked him, and he said, 'Three candles, a box of matches, two loaves of bread, and your siddur.' 'Mine?' I asked him, and he told me he found it in my jacket pocket. Can you imagine? It was the prayer book that belonged to Papa. I always carried it around with me, and Shmuel took the trouble to bring it along. That's the kind of man he was. Of course, the pillowcase was soaked through, oozing black, stinking drops. He held it between his teeth and kept going. The sewer pipe was about seventy or eighty centimeters high, and he crawled on his elbows in order not to bang my head again. It ached something terrible. He went very slowly. It was like a dream. I remember passing the waterfall under Stephan Street. The water dropped six or eight meters there and made a terrific roar in those pipes. But gradually it faded away.

"Then Shmuel stopped. I realized he was exhausted and slipped off his back. I followed him for as long as I could, but there was a sudden rush of water, and I lost him. He was swept away before my eyes. I managed to brace my arms and legs against the pipe, or I would have drowned too. A day or so later . . . I can't be sure . . . it must have rained. The current in the sewers was very strong. I barely managed to keep my head above water.

"After that, I'm not sure what happened. I went off my head. I saw flowers growing down there, in that muck. But they were black. They had black petals. I heard Mama calling me. It was her voice, all right. I'd know it anywhere. She called my name. I wanted to answer her, but was afraid to open my mouth. I was on my back against the pipe, up to my chin in that slime. I was terrified that if I opened my mouth, and a sudden current caught me, I'd drown."

He closes his eyes. "Malka Kravitz eventually found me and took me to her bunker under the cellar at 19 Deitshishe Street, where I spent the rest of the war. We even had a radio and an electric light. We used to sleep during the day, and roam around the sewers at night. Visit other bunkers. We dug a cemetery in the bunker under 9 Gelzer Street and even had a synagogue, where I used to pray. I knew I had been saved for a purpose and tried to prepare myself."

"What purpose?"

He stares at the ceiling.

16 December 1946
Noon

In my office. Leather Jacket, who tells me his name is Nahum, turns out to be an agent of the Haganah. He says, "Your friend Rosenberg, you know, planned the murder of Major Henry in September."

"Henry?"

"The British area security officer."

It all comes back to me: the shots in the night, the explosion of two hundred kilograms of dynamite, and the smoldering debris of the villa on Levinsky Street, which I saw the next morning, where the dying major and the bodies of two Arab policemen were found.

"Was Rosenberg really responsible for that?"

"There's no question of it." Wearing rubber boots, in which he's tucked the ends of his khaki pants, he gives the impression of a cavalryman; all he needs is a braided riding crop. Or at least he tries to give that impression. He has a farmer's hands: red knuckles and dirty fingernails.

He goes on. "Henry was married, you know."

"I had no idea."

"Oh, yes. To a pretty little French girl. She was caught in the blast, of course. No one knows whether she'll make it or not."

"I'm very sorry to hear it."

"I believe you. We know the kind of man you are."

"What kind is that?"

"If you told us where the boy is hiding, we'd pick him up and put him on ice for a while, on a kibbutz in the Galilee."

"He's got a bad infection."

"Has he? Well, we've got a well-equipped infirmary, a good nurse, and a doctor who drops by from Tiberias three times a week. He'll be in good hands. I promise you."

"Is the kibbutz near Tiberias?"

"Close enough."

"Are you a member?" I ask him.

"Yes. I'm in charge of the sheep. Lord, what a stink! You can't get rid of it."

"Rosenberg is armed. He won't be taken alive."

"We have no intention of tangling with him, or any other Jew, unless we have to. Is the boy armed?"

"No, I don't think so."

"Good." He goes to the window and peers down. "God only knows what they're cooking up this time."

I rise and follow him. The middle-aged woman across the street is smoking. Nahum says, "Don't worry about Rosenberg. We'll keep an eye on him. When you make up your mind to tell us where the boy is hiding, tell Guela down there."

It's begun to drizzle. The gray-haired woman turns up the collar of her blue coat.

18 December 1946

I've returned to the cellar alone. The door is unlocked, and my wet shoes squeak as I carefully make my way down the stairs. It suddenly occurs to me that the boy may now have a gun. I pause and strike a match. A brown rat scurries between my feet. The match goes out.

"It's Dr. Spitzer," I call out. "Remember? Rosenberg's friend. I'm all alone. I came by to see how you're coming along."

The boy answers in a hoarse voice, "Of course. Come on down."

"I can't see a damn thing."

"Wait a minute, I'll light my candle," he says. "Come over here and warm up."

Wrapped in his blanket, he is hunched over on the edge of his cot, rubbing his hands over the hissing Primus stove.

"How's this for service?" he asks, thumping his shoe against a jerrican on the floor. "British army-issue gasoline for the stove. Two of our girls stole it last night from an army lorry waiting for a green light on Ben Yehuda."

"Lie down and let me have a look at you."

"No, what's the sense? I'll be leaving here in a day or two anyway, maybe less."

"Leaving?"

"Orders," he says, and asks, "Have you ever killed a man face to face with your bare hands?"

"No."

"I stabbed a Lithuanian man-hunter when I was thirteen. With a bread knife I always carried on me, under my shirt, stuck in my belt."

Pale, sweaty, completely enervated, he lies back with his hands behind his head. His chest is distended. But then he resumes talking with the same passion as before, as if his memory alone remains inexhaustible.

"I stabbed him in the stomach, face to face, in an alley just off Rudnitzer Street, at night. A beautiful spring night, with a full moon. I could see everything. There I was, turning the corner, with a message for Itzik in my pocket, and the Litvak was standing there, lighting a cigarette. He had very bushy blond eyebrows, I remember.

"It was all over in a second. I didn't give him a chance. I threw myself at him and stuck the bread knife into his guts, right up to the hilt. He didn't make a sound. Then I pulled it out, very slowly, and stabbed him again. He was on his knees, holding on to the hilt with both hands. The blood seeped between his fingers. It looked black. Then he fell on his face. His peaked cap rolled off his head.

"I felt happy. That's what the Besht says—may his memory be blessed—'Evil is only the throne of good.'" He sings softly in Yiddish,

> Heavy sheaves of wheat,
> Full of cheerful songs,
> Praise life.
> All its wrongs
> Will be made right.

19 December 1946

I've betrayed the boy's hide-out. This morning I had a few words with poor Guela, who's caught a bad head cold from lurking in that doorway.

"You'd better move tonight," I tell her. "They're up to something."

She sneezes and, with her nose in a handkerchief, turns on her heel toward Allenby, but I stop her. "Do you have the address of my flat?"

"Of course."

"Then ask Nahum to drop by when it's all over, will you?"

She nods, and it's the café on Dizengoff for me, where I order a pint of Johnnie Walker Red, which I can't afford. Two agents of the CID are seated at the next table, to my right, wearing identical clothes: gray flannel trousers and single-breasted blue tweed jackets that bulge from the revolvers they carry in shoulder holsters against their hearts. One of them orders two glasses of whiskey, with a siphon of soda, in a Hebrew which his thick Manchester accent renders almost unintelligible. The waiter, who is a survivor of Sachsenhausen, pretends not to understand.

"The bloody Yid," the agent says in English.

"Forget it," the other one says. "Needn't make a moan of it." He's older, wearier, with a drawn sallow face. "To hell wi' him. Let's pack it in. It's been a long day."

At the door, they put on their trench coats. It's raining again, as if to console them with a memory of home.

I can't help feeling sorry for them. A working knowledge of

Hebrew entitles them to a bonus of five pounds sterling a month, and from the look of their frayed collars and cuffs, they can use it.

1 P.M.

In my flat. Nahum is seated on the chair under the bookshelf with his head in his hands. He's soaked to the skin, and his rubber boots are covered with mud, which he has tracked on my Persian carpet.

"The boy's gone," he says. "Vanished." He looks up. "Do you have something for a headache? My head's splitting."

"What happened?"

"A fuck-up, a complete fuck-up, from beginning to end. Just one of those things. We'd posted a lookout on Hebron Street, opposite the house, to keep an eye out for Rosenberg. Just a kid, but a damn police mobile force, cruising around, picked him up for routine questioning. They took him to the police station on Jaffa Street, checked his papers, which were all in order, of course, asked him a few questions, and then let him go. But by that time, it was too late. Eli and I arrived at Hebron Street at exactly ten P.M., as we'd planned. The lookout, of course, wasn't there, but we decided to take a chance. We went into the back yard, but I knew something was wrong. The cellar door was wide open, banging in the wind. Eli shined his flashlight down there, but the place was empty. A cot, a table, a Primus, and a jerrican of gasoline. There was a rat on the table gnawing on a candle. The boy was gone."

"Rosenberg took him. He's got special plans for that boy."

What good can come of it?

THE CRAZY OLD MAN

The old man lives in the same apartment on Jaffa Road in Jerusa-lem. He's in his late eighties and blinded by a cataract in his left eye, but when I saw him last, about a week after the liberation of the Old City, he was on his way, alone, to pray at the Wall. He recognized me immediately—or so I thought—but after a few minutes' conversation on the street I realized that he confused me with Uzi because he asked if I still lived in Haifa. I let it pass, and chatted for a while. He still lived with his daughter, he said, who was married to a captain in the paratroops, and had two children. His son-in-law had fought and been wounded in the fight for the Old City, making a dash across the crest of the Temple Mount toward the Dome of the Rock.

"What's his name?" I asked.

"Seligman."

"Raphael?" I asked, and he answered in Yiddish, "Yes. You know him?"

"We've met."

He peered at me with his good eye; at my unshaven face and civilian clothes—a filthy white shirt and blue trousers I was wear-ing for an Intelligence job I'd just finished in the Old City.

"So you know Raphael," he said.

"He's a good soldier."

"Is he?"

"Where was he hit?" I asked.

"In the right arm."

Then he said, "I must go and pray for him, and ask forgiveness." And off he went, wearing a black felt hat with a wide brim, a long black gabardine coat, and those knee-length white stockings. In his right hand he carried a ragged blue-velvet bag embroidered with a gold Star of David, for his prayer shawl. He was the same. Nothing had changed for him in almost twenty years. I resisted an impulse to run upstairs to take a look at his apartment, imagining that that, too, had remained the same, with its wicker chairs and that hideous sideboard made from teak and inlaid with mother-of-pearl that he had bought from some Arab when he first came to the country from Russia in 1912. Instead, I strolled up King George Street and, to get out of the sun, had a cup of bitter coffee in the Café Vienna.

That afternoon, driving back to GHQ in Tel Aviv, I passed Dan buses, private cars, captured Jordanian Ford trucks with Arab license plates, and even a Russian Jeep taken from the Syrians. They were all packed with people heading for the Wall. The rest of the Old City was still closed to civilians because of snipers and mines. I thought about Uzi, who died in 1953 in a car accident on the Tel Aviv–Haifa road, and the two Arab prisoners.

At the time, in July 1948, during the Ten Days' Fighting just before the second truce, Uzi and I were with the Haganah's Intelligence in Jerusalem, assigned to interrogate prisoners and gather information for the coordinated attack that was to be made on the Old City.

The plan was simple: a simultaneous breakthrough from the north through the New Gate by a unit of the Irgun, and from the south, by the Haganah, near the Zion Gate. The Old City wall is four yards thick here, but we had high hopes that we'd be able to breach it with a new explosive that we had never tried before. As it turned out, the stuff hardly scratched the wall's surface, and the plan failed. So, in the end, what we did was useless.

Uzi and I had been detailed to find out the exact number and disposition of the Arab forces around the Zion Gate from two Jordanian legionnaires who had been captured the day before. We had twelve hours to get the information out of them, so we took them to my apartment, which I had used as a "drop" for ammunition during the Mandate and where I now did most of my work. It was one room on the second floor, right across the hall from the old man and his daughter. They didn't bother me much. The old man was busy praying, and the girl, who was about twelve or

thirteen, was very shy. Only once, in the last month of th
date, the old man invited me into his apartment for a glass

"I insist," he told me. "The kettle's on the stove. There, you
hear? Already boiling. Sit down. I have no lemon. Sugar?"

He blew into his steaming glass and, with a spoonful of sugar
already on his tongue, took a sip and smacked his lips. "Ah. That's
a pleasure. Sugar on the tongue." He smiled. "For me, it somehow
never tastes as good in the glass. A habit from the Old Country.
But you, of course, were born here, weren't you?"

"Yes, in Tel Aviv."

"Tel Aviv. Is that so?" he said. "You're lucky."

"You think so?"

"I know so. You see, this is your chance. Not mine. Not an old
Jew like me who came here to pray for forgiveness and die, but
yours. My daughter Chanele's and yours, if you understand me."

"Thanks for the tea, but I have to go out. It's almost curfew."

"No, no, wait. Just one minute. You must listen to me for just one
minute and try to understand." He began to sweat. "The Exile,
you see, the real Exile is that we learned to endure it," he went
on. "Rabbi Hanokh, may he rest in peace, once said that, and he
was right. But it's all over now. I can feel it. I look at you and even
my little Chanele, my shy little Chanele, who dreams of becoming
a courier for the Haganah . . . Can you believe that? It's true. At
twelve. That pious child . . . All of you who were born here have
had enough and will have your State. For you, the Exile is over.
Not that it wasn't deserved." He raised a forefinger. "Oh, no.
Never for one moment think that. We sinned and were punished
for it. It was just. But He has relented, you see, may His Name be
blessed forever and ever, and, in His mercy, has given you one
more chance. You must be careful. Very, very careful.

"When I was ten years old, there was a pogrom in my town, near
Kiev. Ten Jews were killed and three were wounded. A Russian
blacksmith, called Big Kolya, murdered his Jewish neighbor, a
woman named Sarah Effros, with whom he had lived in peace for
forty years. Then came the pogrom. He got drunk and strangled
her. When he sobered up, he went back to work at his forge, as
if nothing had happened. That's a goy for you! Goyim are killers!
Not us."

We had twelve hours to get the information from the prisoners.

It wasn't much time. We started in about nine at night, working them over according to the system that Uzi and I had found to be effective twice before. It was nothing unusual: threats, alternating with promises, and, above all, keeping them on their feet and awake. Uzi and I took turns, an hour each, while the other covered them with my Beretta. We kept them awake with slaps across the face. Even so, just before dawn the older one, who was a lieutenant, passed out on the floor.

Uzi slapped him. I hit the younger one in the mouth with my fist, and split his upper lip. We let him bleed. He was about twenty, a private, still in his khaki uniform, with the red-and-white checkered kaffiah, the headdress of the Legion, wrapped around his neck like a kerchief. His mouthful of blood scared the hell out of him. You could tell by the look in his eyes. He was afraid to spit it out and mess up the floor. Finally he took off the kaffiah and, crumpling it up in his hand, spat into that. Then he puked in it. His lip swelled up and made it hard for him to talk.

"I don't know," he kept repeating. "I swear I don't know. I have no idea."

The lieutenant, who had a swollen right cheek, never made a sound. He was about thirty, and good-looking, with a deep cleft in his chin and a carefully clipped little mustache. The British officers who had trained him had done a good job. He was a professional soldier and proud of it. He stood at parade rest, in the middle of the room, with his hands clasped behind his back and his feet spread about a yard apart, according to regulations. That was the way he had fallen asleep.

"The kid," Uzi whispered to me. "Our only chance is the kid."

He punched him in the stomach, and the boy doubled up and fell, knocking over a small table with his shoulder. The coffee cups and a half bottle of brandy shattered on the tile floor.

All of a sudden, there was a pounding on the door that didn't stop until I opened it a crack and saw the old man. He had phylacteries bound to his forehead. We had interrupted his morning prayers.

"What is it? What's happening here?" he asked me in Yiddish.

"Go away," I told him. "It's none of your business."

I tried shutting the door in his face, but he stuck one foot inside and with surprising strength threw it wide open.

"Who is it?" Uzi asked.

"Rosenblum," I told him. "From across the hall."

"Well, get rid of him."

The boy, who was still on the floor, raised himself up on his elbows and stared at the old man.

"Get him out of here," Uzi repeated. In the distance, maybe three or four blocks away, up Ben Yehuda Street, there was an explosion. The windows rattled. The Arabs were shelling us from the Old City. As a matter of fact, when I look back on it now, they had been shelling and mortaring us all night long, at irregular intervals. We were just impervious to it; only our bodies reacted instinctively every time there was an explosion. Everyone—even the lieutenant, I noticed with satisfaction—contracted his shoulders and ducked his head. Once, about seven in the morning, when an ambulance clanged up Jaffa Road in the direction of the King David, I went to the window to take a look. The street was strewn with rubble: broken glass, glittering in the fresh light, rolls of toilet paper, the burned-out wreck of an old Packard sedan, and fragments of the beautiful, rose-colored stone, quarried from the Judean hills, from which the houses of the New City are built.

The old man unwrapped his phylacteries from his forehead.

"You were born here?" he asked Uzi.

"What of it?"

"Were you?"

"Yes, in Haifa, where I live. So what?"

"And you, if I remember, in Tel Aviv," the old man said to me. "Yes."

He slammed the door shut behind him and stood there, with his arms folded across his chest. He said, "Let them go."

Maybe, from the tone of his voice, the boy guessed what the old man intended; anyhow, he tried to smile, with his swollen lip. The lieutenant yawned, delicately covering his mouth with his hand.

Then the old man spouted from Isaiah, in a hoarse, singsong voice. " 'No lion shall be there, nor any ravenous beast shall go up thereon, it will not be found there; but the redeemed shall walk there.' Let them go," he said.

Uzi dragged the boy to his feet by the collar and hit him in the stomach again. He retched but didn't bring anything up.

"Well?"

The boy shook his head. Uzi hit him again and let him drop on his back to the floor.

"Listen to me," the old man said. "You must listen to me."

Uzi and I took turns beating the boy while the lieutenant and the old man watched.

"Don't know," he mumbled. "Don't know."

It was possible that he was telling the truth, but we had less than an hour left, and we had to make sure. Uzi hit him in the stomach once more, and then we both had the same idea at the same time. I had unconsciously scratched the nape of my neck with the muzzle of the Beretta. The lieutenant, who was yawning again, lowered his hand, took a deep breath, and straightened up. He understood too.

"Shoot him," Uzi said in Arabic.

I released the Beretta's safety catch and aimed with both hands at the lieutenant's face. The old man grabbed the barrel, and I was so surprised, I let go. The lieutenant jumped to the right, toward the window, but was off balance, and landed on his knees. The first round, which hit his chest, spun him around, and threw him on his back. Then the old man walked over and shot him in the right eye.

The boy cried, "Yah Allah!"—"Oh God!"—and told us what we wanted to know. Uzi took notes on a pad of yellow paper. The old man gave me back the gun, and said, "Let the blood be on my head. I don't matter. But you were born here. Take care! The Holy One, blessed be He, has given your generation the Land of Israel. Be worthy of His gift. Keep your hands clean."

FORCING THE END

Rabbi Jacobi stands in front of my desk, pulling the tuft of white beard that sprouts beneath his underlip.

He says, "All I want is your permission to leave the city, go to Yavneh, open up a school there, and teach."

"Yes, I understand, Rabbi, but unfortunately, under the circumstances, I must refuse you permission."

"What circumstances?"

"For one thing, you'll be safer here."

"Really?" he asks. "Look out the window and tell me what you see."

"Jaffa Road."

"Look again."

I rise to my feet.

We're in the desert. Mount Zion is bare, its eastern slope lit by the sun. Huge, yellowish limestone boulders, tinged with red, cast shadows on the slopes. The ruins of buildings? It's impossible to tell. A jackal pisses on the big rock beneath my window.

The rabbi says, "You're looking at the Holy City through my eyes."

"The past?"

"The future, too. They're one and the same."

"Impossible."

He covers his face, saying, "God help us, it's true."

I look out the window again. A Sammael, one of our newest, self-propelled nuclear missiles, roars up Jaffa Road toward the Russian Compound.

Jacobi twists that tuft of beard between the thumb and forefinger of his right hand. Is he a hypnotist? I read over his dossier, open on my desk, once again. He was born in Jerusalem in 1917 and was ordained at the age of nineteen. After that, for twelve years, he was the rabbi of the small town of Arav in the southern Galilee, where he also worked as a clerk in the local post office because he refused any remuneration for teaching Torah. His wife died last year, and he lost his only son at the age of sixteen to nephritis. The boy was also a precociously brilliant scholar, of whom his father said at his death, "I am consoled by the fact that my son, may his memory be blessed, fulfilled the purpose for which man was created—the study of the Holy Law."

For the last eight years, Jacobi has lived in Jerusalem, teaching a select group of students in a small Talmud Torah on Adani Street. He has been in constant conflict with the rabbinate over its acquisition of extensive property, and with the government over its policy of retaliatory raids for terrorist attacks.

My secretary, Dora, whose husband was killed two years ago by an Arab grenade while serving on reserve duty in Gaza, comes into my office and whispers excitedly in my ear, "We attack on Sunday, at dawn."

"How do you know?"

"Yoram's sister heard it from her husband."

"Who's her husband?"

"The pilot."

"What's the matter with you? You know how tight security is. It's just another rumor."

She adds without conviction, "Yoram's sister swears it's the truth," and sighs. She has aged extraordinarily in the last two years; her lips are wrinkled.

"There's still time," Jacobi says. "Not much, but enough. At least enough for me to go to Yavneh, open my school, and plant a few lemon trees. They're very delicate. I love the odor of the blossoms. Sweet but spicy." He goes to the door and says. "Tell me the truth. Do you honestly believe that this time we'll achieve a lasting peace?"

"Absolutely."

"By force of arms?"

"Yes."

He opens the door. "Did you know that lemons turn yellow only after they've been picked? It's a fact. They remain green and bitter on the tree. You have to store them for months before they ripen and turn yellow."

"Not anymore," Dora says. "A specially heated storage plant forces them to ripen in four or five days."

"As ripe as this?" he asks, holding up a yellow lemon in his right hand.

Then closing his eyes and inhaling deeply, he recites the traditional benediction, " 'Blessed art Thou—the Eternal, our God, King of the Universe—who hath given fragrance unto fruit.' " He smiles, and says, "This was picked from a tree four days ago and then stored at exactly twenty-two degrees Centigrade." He twirls it in the air.

"Why, you could say it's like the world: cut off from its source, and ignorant of its condition. But just think! A slight malfunction of a machine in that storage plant, or a human error, causes the temperature to rise a few degrees, and look! The lemon turns brown and shrivels up. It's rotten! See?"

He hands it to Dora, who throws it into the wastebasket next to my desk. The rabbi asks her, "Is it true about you and your brother?" She doesn't answer. She and her brother Eliazar are reputed members of The Knives, a new, illegal organization allegedly responsible for the murder of the novelist Uri Ben Ami, who advocated making peace with the Arabs by restoring to them the Occupied Territories.

The rabbi asks me, "Won't you change your mind and give me permission to go to Yavneh with my students and teach?"

"I can't."

He shakes my hand, and says, "Peace!"

"Peace be unto thee!"

Friday afternoon while I'm having my glass of tea and a butter cookie, I glance out of the window and see four soldiers, armed with submachine guns, patrolling the street. Each has inserted a thirty-round magazine into his weapon, behind the trigger guard, and has taped another magazine at right angles to the first, to facilitate rapid reloading. Their footfalls are muffled by the sandbags that last night were heaped up, waist high, against the buildings.

Then, at a command from their sergeant, they break rank, to allow a funeral procession to pass down the center of the street. Four bearded men, dressed in black caftans, are carrying an unpainted pine coffin on their shoulders. Behind them are three howling women, who wear black shawls over their heads.

"Who is it?" I shout. "Who has died?"

The howling women rake their cheeks with their fingernails.

"Answer me!" I yell louder, and one of the bearded pallbearers shouts back, "Our master, Rabbi Jacobi, the Light of the World."

"When did he die?"

"This morning."

"Where are you taking the body?"

"To Arav."

"Why Arav?"

Dora, who is standing behind me, says, "I'll check it out."

She returns a few minutes later, and says, "It's O.K. They're burying him in Arav next to his son."

"Who authorized them to leave Jerusalem?"

"What's his name? Oh, you know who I mean. That Litvak from the Ministry of Interment who dyes his hair."

"Kovner."

"That's the one."

Next morning, Shmelke Kalb, from the Ministry of Tourism, bursts into my office, waving a newspaper.

"Have you read about Jacobi?"

"What about him?"

"He's escaped to Yavneh with a bunch of his students."

"What're you talking about? The man's dead. I saw his coffin."

"That's how his students smuggled him out of Jerusalem—in a sealed coffin. It's all in the paper, along with a manifesto he wrote for his new school in Yavneh."

Kalb reads aloud:

> We shall be as the disciples of Aaron, loving peace, pursuing peace, and teaching Torah which alone sustains the Jews who, if they faithfully follow its Holy Principles, will be redeemed by them, and then redeem all mankind, in God's good time . . .

Dora has come to the door; Kalb lowers his voice: "Kovner has disappeared."

At one—during critical times like these, we grab a sandwich for lunch at the office—Dora turns on the radio for the latest news.

". . . which will demand from each of us the greatest sacrifice . . . credence, which, although . . . New York . . ."

I can catch only a word now and then because columns of Sammaels, rattling the windowpanes, have been roaring up the street for the last two hours. Then they pass and I hear the announcer say that Rabbi Jacobi's body, spattered with blood, was discovered in Yavneh early this morning in front of a vegetarian restaurant on the Rishon-Lezion road. A preliminary coroner's report has established that the distinguished religious leader was stabbed once through the heart with a butcher knife, and died instantly, between 2 and 3 A.M. The district superintendent of police reports that no fingerprints were found on the weapon, but he has been quoted that he is confident that the criminal or criminals will soon be apprehended because of a peculiar aspect of the case. The distinguished rabbi's jaws were pried open after his death, and a green lemon was stuck in the corpse's mouth. . . .

Dora laughs.

THE ELEPHANT
AND MY JEWISH PROBLEM:
A JOURNAL

Late this afternoon, two German lesbians barged into the garden. They made it as far as the greenhouse, where Bettyann was watering the cucumbers. The older one, who spoke English, said they'd driven down from London just to see Virginia's studio. Then she added, "Give us five minutes." An hour and a half later, while they were nosing around the potted cacti in the conservatory attached to the back of the house, Dan threw them out.

After supper, he nailed a typewritten note to the front gate:

**MONK'S HOUSE IS INHABITED. WE APPRECIATE YOUR
RESPECT FOR OUR PRIVACY**

He and Bettyann, who have rented the house since May, have had it with the tourists. Last Monday, a graduate student from Stanford tried to make off with one of the painted saucers, signed Vanessa Bell, on the shelf in the sitting room. Bettyann had invited him in. He was carrying two paperbacks: *The Death of the Moth and Other Essays,* and *To the Lighthouse.*

I'm re-reading Quentin Bell's biography of Virginia—or was until this morning, when Marilyn snatched it out of my hands. We squabbled by the fish pond, in the garden, where the drought has turned the grass brown. The heat made me drowsy; the flies drove Marilyn inside. There's also a plague of ladybugs. Just before lunch, in the kitchen, I grabbed the book from the table, and read all afternoon.

At sundown, I'm at the fish pond again for another look at the two lead busts on the low flint wall. Leonard is on the left: an old man with a full head of hair and sunken cheeks. His eyes are almost shut. At the other end is Virginia, who wrote in her journal, "Work and love and Jews in Putney take it out of me."

Kate, our six-year-old, has recently become a disciple of Schweitzer. Twice today, on those red-brick paths in the garden, between the rosebushes and the weeds, she had a fit because I accidentally stepped on a ladybug. And at supper, as Dan sliced the roast pork, she asked Marilyn, "What was pork when it was alive?"

"A pig."

"Who cut off the legs and the head?"

"The butcher. Do you want a baked potato?"

"I don't want no pork," she said.

Dan swims a couple of hours every afternoon at the University of Sussex, near Brighton, where he's a Visiting Research Fellow. Jonathan, his eight-year-old, plays cricket in the paddock near the barley field up the road. He picked it up from his buddy, Giles, a kid the same age whose parents have a summer cottage in the village.

Back at four-thirty, Dan goes straight to Leonard's study on the third floor, where he's finishing a paper on the history of eugenics. A few minutes later, the two sweaty kids arrive: Giles with a cricket bat on his shoulder, Jonathan with a hard rubber ball. Kate trails after them to the table on my left at the end of the sitting room, where there's a game called Escape from Colditz in a red box. Bettyann bought it Saturday in Lewes.

The dice rattle. Giles says, "You're the German guard," and Kate bounces the ball on the stone floor. I put Bell's book beside me on the sofa. Jonathan, who's facing me, picks up a laminated card from the top of a pack on his right and looks at it. The back is red; there's a black swastika in the middle.

Dan says, "The Nazis set back the study of eugenics for decades; it wasn't respectable after the Nürnberg Laws. Now, of course, the possibility of scientific genetic engineering makes it very important."

The lights are on in The Holly. We elbow our way to the bar. Denis, who runs the pub, has put us on to Super Lager, in a brown beer bottle, which has a kick like whiskey. Cynthia, his American wife, pours a pint for him in an engraved pewter mug and takes over for a few minutes so we can chat. We come around to the Olympics in Montreal, where it's raining, and Denis says, "It's the winters there that's hell. I've seen snowdrifts on Crescent Street seven feet high."

The former manager of a rock band, he also knows New York, Chicago, San Francisco, L.A., and Mansfield, Ohio, where he remembers an old log fort.

"Cyn and me met at a party in Detroit," he tells us. "I had us booked there for three weeks at a spot called The Jack Flash. It's gone now."

We order another round.

"Does warm beer bother you?" Cynthia asks me.

"No, I like it."

"It bothered me a long time."

Dan asks Denis, "Did you watch Naber swim the two-hundred-meter freestyle yesterday?"

"No, I missed it."

"Me, too. I won't be able to watch him Saturday either, damn it. I have to go to London."

"More's the pity, seeing as how these Olympics are the last they'll be for a long time to come."

"Not so long. 1980."

"Aye, but scheduled where?"

"In Moscow."

"That's the point," he says. "They'll be none in Moscow then. You mark my words."

"Why not?" Dan asks. "What's to prevent it?"

"The Jewish bankers. They rule the world."

Friday afternoon
6 P.M.

Quentin Bell, his wife, and his eighteen-year-old daughter here for drinks. Kate goes upstairs to watch TV with Jonathan. His fourteen-year-old sister, Beth, slips out of the room with a book under her arm: *The Wrath of the Vikings.*

The rest of us sit facing the mantelpiece on which Virginia left a suicide note. Bell remarks to Dan that Leonard's mother and sister, who lived in Putney, visited him here once or twice a week for years.

I ask, "How did Virginia take it?"

"Not very well, I'm afraid."

"Because they were Jews?"

"I'm afraid so," says Bell.

Marilyn says, "Hugh is like the Jewish zoology student."

Bell: "Pardon?"

"The zoology class is assigned a paper on the elephant. The Englishman writes 'Hunting the Elephant.' The Frenchman, 'The Love Life of the Elephant.' The Jewish student turns in a paper, 'The Elephant and the Jewish Problem.' "

Bell: "I see. Well, I dare say that when she was young, Virginia had a Jewish problem. Leonard, too, if the truth be told. It's a common English ailment. It doesn't mean much. Leonard decided to commit suicide if the Germans invaded. Virginia was determined to do it with him. They hoarded petrol. They intended to gas themselves by running the motor of their car in the locked garage beneath the house."

We stroll in the garden. The inscription on the marble plaque beneath the bust of Virginia is adapted from *The Waves*:

> Death is the enemy. Against you, I will
> fling myself unvanquished and unyielding
> —O Death.

Saturday

A plowman's lunch this afternoon at The Holly for 60 p: fresh lettuce, two sliced tomatoes, a thick wedge of cheddar, a spoonful of chutney, a chunk of bread from a round loaf, two patties of butter wrapped in yellow foil. Perched on a high stool at the bar, I also have two pints of India Pale Ale on draft. Cynthia waves a bee away from the chutney and asks, "Where you from?"

"New York."

"I grew up in Hamtramck. Do you know Detroit at all?"

Denis says, "I understand you're a writer. Staying at Monk's House must mean a lot to you. Dan tells me a novel of yours has just been published in England. What's it about?"

"Jews."

"Jews! Is that so? So you're Jewish, then?"

"I am."

"Well done!"

"Thank you."

"Not at all, old chap. Let me put a head on that beer."

Late Monday afternoon, Bettyann and I went shopping in Lewes—a ten-minute drive. Beth came along to return a pile of overdue books to the public library. We left her browsing among the shelves in the main reading room. At the fishmonger on the Cliff High Street, Bettyann bought a six-pound salmon trout for supper and seven smoked mackerel for tomorrow's lunch. On the way back, she and I ate one of the mackerel with our fingers.

Kate, like my mother, has a particularly acute sense of smell. She made me wash my hands before reading aloud to her from *Mr. Topsy-Turvy* in the sitting room. The boys, who were playing Escape from Colditz, chased her away. She sat in my lap, sucking her thumb, while I read,

> That day, Mr. Topsy-Turvy did all sorts of topsy-turvy things. He walked backward across a street crossing and caused an enormous traffic jam.

"Read more!" she said.

Giles yelled, "I'm out! I made it! I win!" and because it was an excuse to put down *Mr. Topsy-Turvy* for a minute, I looked at him.

He said, "Excuse me," in a lowered voice.

"That's O.K."

"I was the British POW, you see, and escaped."

"So I gathered."

He asked, "Were you in the war?"

"No, but I remember it very well."

Kate said, "I have to tinkle."

"My father was in London during the Blitz," Giles said. "His nanny lost an eye."

"The Germans did bad things. The people who owned this house, for example, made up their minds to kill themselves if the Germans invaded England."

"Why is that?" Giles asked.

"Because the Germans would have killed them. They killed

millions of people in Europe during the war—men, women, kids your age. They stripped them naked and packed them in rooms maybe twice this size, but with thick concrete walls and steel doors. Then they locked them in and gassed them."

Giles said, "They were only Jews."

IN THE REIGN OF PEACE

By three-thirty, when we finished work in the orchard, there was almost nothing left of the mouse: a blotch of dried blood on the flagstones, to which a little tuft of fur was still stuck. The bones, ground to powder, had been blown away by the wind. All the ants were gone. Chaim said nothing. It was Friday, and we had quit early so that he could return home to Kiriat Shemona before sundown to attend the service in the Moroccan synagogue there. And as always at the coming of the Sabbath, he solemnly shook my hand.

"Shabbat shalom."

"Yes, and to you too," I told him. "A peaceful Sabbath."

With the eight other workers hired by the kibbutz, he boarded the truck outside the communal dining hall. They were all recent North African or Iraqi immigrants; not yet so proficient in Hebrew, they jabbered away in Arabic, all excited by the anticipation of a good meal and a day of rest. Only Chaim, who secured the chain of the tailgate, remained silent. For a moment, squinting up at him in the sun, I had the impression that I was looking at him through the eyes of a goy, just as my grandfather must have been seen by the Poles in Krakow. And with the same hatred. The truck started up, the chain rattled, and Chaim waved. With the other hand, he held on to his hat. It was because of that hat he always wore—a battered green fedora, stained with sweat—his thick black beard, and his sidelocks, which he tucked up above his ears —everything with which he set himself apart.

At seven, my wife and I put Ethan to bed in the children's house.

He's four, and wants to sleep with us in our room, but rules are rules.

"Shabbat shalom."

The greeting, exchanged in the twilight, by the kibbutz members, meant nothing. We would work tomorrow, like any other day —harder. The cows would be milked and the eggs collected, and we would begin picking the apples. It's the one thing about us that Chaim still refuses to believe.

"Jews working on the Sabbath? Ah, now you're joking with me," he once said.

"Haven't you?"

"No, thanks be to God."

"Never? Not even once in Rabat?"

"Never," he said, and in his guttural accent, which rasped in the back of his throat, he told me something about his life in Morocco.

The Sabbath had preserved him. It had been his only respite from the work that had earned him barely enough to keep himself and his family alive: carrying hundredweight sacks of charcoal through those narrow, reeking streets to the Arab ironmongers.

On the Sabbath, he remained in the shack near the old entrance to the ghetto, where he lived in one room with his wife and six kids. For the most part, he slept away the day on the earthen floor. Once in a while he would be awakened by a wailing child and rouse himself to eat the cold remains of the Sabbath feast from the night before: a lamb pilaf, in which the fat and the rice had congealed. He ate only with the fingers of his right hand, like an Arab, and his children would lick them clean, one by one. It was all their mother would allow. Today the meat, even the fat, she told them, was only for their father. What would happen to them all if, God forbid, their father lost his strength?

Chaim could never keep awake for long. The heat and the buzzing of the flies made him sleepy. He always tried to recite at least a portion of the Sabbath prayer before he passed out again. "Exalt ye the Lord our God . . ."

Impossible. He was never once able to finish it. He sank back on the pile of greasy rags he used as a pillow. Just before his eyes closed, he saw one of his naked kids, on all fours, sniffing at his right hand—Masouda, his youngest daughter, whom the others always pushed aside.

"And now?" I asked him.

"Ah, now, praise His Name, I can pray in the synagogue for as long as I like."

"And does Masouda get enough to eat?"

"She's dead. She died two years ago, when we all caught the spotted fever." He spat between his fingers to avert the evil eye. "My wife lost all her hair. All of it, even between her legs."

He told me very little about his life in this country. He had been here almost a year, living in Kiriat Shemona. I could imagine the rest: the three-room flat, provided by the government for a nominal rent, and everything else bought on credit—the television set on which he watched American movies, dubbed in Arabic, broadcast from Beirut, the refrigerator, the gas stove, maybe a coffee table with a Formica top, and even a bed.

He worked wherever he could: repairing the northern frontier road, or for some kibbutz, like ours, that was always short-handed. He had been with us for a week. Unlike other Moroccans we had hired over the years—petit-bourgeois tradesmen, or those who wanted to be—he wasn't ashamed of working with his hands. He enjoyed it and had an instinctive feeling for tools: the long-handled, two-handed shears with which I taught him to prune the excess branches from the apple trees.

"That's it," I told him. "Gently, so you don't tear the bark. And not too near the trunk."

"What's that?"

"That's very important. It's white paint with lead in it."

"What for?"

"You must always smear it on the wound to prevent fungus infection."

"Fungus?"

"A kind of disease."

"Ah . . ."

And then, after he watched me for a moment, "Does the tree feel any pain?"

"No."

"But it gets sick just like us?"

"Exactly."

"I see," he said, and he stared in astonishment at the Baldwin apple tree that shared our fate.

In the days that followed, he would shut his shears and stare in the same way, with an open mouth, at the whole world of which he was now a part: the rotting apples, scattered on the earth, that swarmed with bees; the pear trees in the south orchard, with their glossy, pointed leaves; a yellow butterfly; a mouse scurrying through the dry grass.

By the end of the second week, at the beginning of August, it was obvious that there was going to be a bumper crop, the best in over three years.

Chaim said, "Praise His Name, you'll be a rich man."

"No, not me. It belongs to the kibbutz."

"This orchard isn't yours?"

"Of course not. I thought you understood that."

"Ai, habibi, no, I didn't know." For the first time between us, he had used the Arabic endearment, only for lovers and friends. And then he whispered, "Tell me. How much do they pay you?"

"Nothing. I don't need any money. The kibbutz gives me everything I need."

"Free?"

"In return for my work."

"I don't understand."

"It's very simple." But I was too hot, too tired, and too hungry to go on. It was one o'clock, time for lunch.

We walked up the flagstone path, between the azalea bushes and the lilacs, toward the dining hall. Under the eucalyptus trees, I tried again.

"We share everything equally here. Can you understand that?"

"Oh, yes," he said. "Why?"

"Because it's just."

"Just?" He pricked up his ears at the word. It was a word he finally seemed to understand. Not from personal experience—those sacks of charcoal, the famished child smelling his hand—but perhaps from his Bible. The half-forgotten phrases came back to me from my childhood. "The way of the just is as shining light." "The path of the just . . ."

He said dubiously, "Ah, yes . . ."

At the sink, in the dining hall, while he carefully washed his hands, he muttered the benediction under his breath. And at the table, with closed eyes, he prayed again over a mug of water, a tomato, and two thick slices of rye bread. It was the only food of ours he ever touched. Even our white cheese was suspect. A plate of beef liver and noodles, set before him, made him avert his face. He chewed the dry bread and looked mournfully about him at the tables crowded with sunburned men and stout women wearing shorts and heavy boots.

"No one here is kosher?" he asked me.

"No one."

"Not one of you believes in God?"

"Not one."

"Or in the Messiah?"

"No."

"You don't believe in the coming of the Messiah?"

With my mouth stuffed with noodles, I shook my head, and he stared at me, appalled.

I should have known. It wasn't just the Sabbath which had sustained him in Rabat—that lamb pilaf and the few extra hours of sleep—but that absurd hope. He must have believed in the same kind of things as my grandfather: that, at the End of Days, when the Messiah comes, He'll raise the dead and restore the sacred cruse of oil to the Temple, which He'll rebuild with a wave of His hand.

For the rest of the afternoon, as we laid plastic irrigation pipes between the pear trees in the south orchard, Chaim was silent. Then, at five, when we quit for the day, he asked me, "You don't believe in redemption?"

It was in the same voice as before, with the same tone of incredulity and sadness, but now hoarse from fatigue.

"Yes," I told him. "I suppose, in a way, that I do. I believe that one day everyone will live like this."

"Like what?"

"Sharing everything."

"Is that all?"

"What more would you want?"

He said nothing. The sweat streamed down his face. His damp

beard, which clung to the contour of his jaw, revealed a receding chin. It was unexpected and gratifying, the suggestion of some hidden weakness—an inconstancy—bred in the man's very bones.

By the second week of September, the apples were ripe. On Wednesday afternoon I went into Kiriat Shemona to our cooperative cold-storage plant and arranged for the disposition of our crop. Beginning Saturday, for eight days, we would ship and store six tons a day. The entire work force of the kibbutz would be mobilized to pick the apples. Each member would be required to work an extra twenty-four hours in the orchard. We would be at it from 4 A.M. to 6 P.M. in that September heat. Even the kids over thirteen would have to lend a hand.

On Friday, at noon, I went into the co-op again and brought back the big GMC with the electric winch and the aluminum bins in which the apples are packed. Chaim was waiting for me outside the dining hall. He had been squatting on his heels in the shadow of the overhanging roof. Now he stood up.

"What is it?" I asked him. "What's the matter?"

"Come and see."

I followed him down the flagstone path toward the orchard. It was almost two, the hottest time of the day. A gust of wind, blowing across the lawn, brought with it the smell of dry manure.

"Quick," he called out, breaking into a run.

Under the eucalyptus trees, he suddenly stopped and squatted down again on his haunches, leaning forward with his hands between his knees.

"There," he said. "You see? And still alive."

It was a mouse, a field mouse, with a white underside, which had evidently come up through a hole in the concrete between two flagstones and gotten stuck halfway. The forepaws waved in the air.

"What about it?"

"Look closer."

I knelt down beside him. The forepaws waved and the head jerked up and down. I could see a black ant, its antennae waving, in the right nostril. The mouse was covered with ants, hundreds of them, that swarmed over that palpitating white chest, the coarse, tawny fur between the eyes, and in the large ears bristling with short hairs. The ears were oozing blood. A bright drop, flung wide by a jerk of the head, landed on the toe of my shoe.

"Kill it," I told Chaim. "It's being eaten alive. What are you waiting for?"

"I tried," he said. "Listen."

We stood up, and he raised his right foot. The mouse screeched, faintly, thinly, but audibly, even above the rustle of the wind in the eucalyptus leaves above our heads.

"Did you hear that?" said Chaim. "It knows."

"It's because of your shadow."

"My what?"

"The shadow of your foot, which it mistakes for the shadow of a dangerous animal or a bird. A hawk perhaps."

"Is that so?"

"Be quick," I told him.

After lunch, we drove the big GMC down to the orchard and unloaded the aluminum bins.

"Why didn't you kill it right away?" I asked him.

"I wanted you to see it."

"Why?"

"Ai, habibi . . ." He removed the last bin from the back of the truck and added, "Things like that must happen all the time, don't you think?"

"I imagine so."

"Yes," he said. "But not in the reign of peace."

"The reign of peace?"

"When the Messiah comes." He put the bin down and raised his forefinger. "Not then."

The finger wagged, and I understood. On the flagstone path, under the eucalyptus trees, he had shown me what he expected to be redeemed.

LAMENTATIONS

"I'm three months pregnant," said Elana. "Uri is going to be a father."

Yigael, who had been waiting for this all through dinner, drank off the rest of his brandy, and said, "He told me. Mazel tov."

"Thank you. I found out the day after you were called up, but I couldn't decide whether to write him about it or not. He had enough to worry about out there."

"You did the right thing. It made him very happy."

"Did it?" she asked eagerly.

"Very."

"I'm so glad. I couldn't tell from his last letter. He asked me to marry him, of course, but almost as an afterthought. Most of it was about one of his men who had been blinded by a piece of shrapnel the day before."

"Avner Levi."

"That's the one."

"He and Uri were friends at law school," said Yigael. "Believe me, under the circumstances, Uri was very happy. He asked me to be his best man."

"Then do," Elana said.

"I don't understand."

"It's very simple. I want the child to have his name, so I spoke with the chaplain of your outfit, who fixed it with the rabbinate. We're getting married next Thursday afternoon at Bet Hakerem."

"In the cemetery?"

"Over his grave," Elana said. "I insisted on it."

Yigael tried to imagine the scene. Would there be a chuppah?

A canopy erected over the mound of fresh earth? And who would speak for the dead? Slip the ring on the girl's finger and then smash the glass underfoot?

"Can you make it?" she asked.

"Yes, I think so. I'll get Ginzberg to take my afternoon class."

"Good. It'll be a very small affair. Just the immediate family and you," she said, licking her spoon.

"How about a cup of coffee?"

"It's too warm. But another ice cream would be nice."

"More chocolate?"

"Make it vanilla this time."

"Waiter, a dish of vanilla ice cream," Yigael called out. "And bring me another brandy. A double."

"Some water, too."

"And two glasses of cold water."

"I'm simply ravenous all the time," Elana said.

"No morning sickness?"

"Not a bit of it. The only symptom I have is sore breasts. My nipples are very tender."

The waiter carried the dish of ice cream, the snifter of brandy, and two glasses of cloudy water to the table on a big aluminum tray. He was about fifty, tall, stooped, and surprisingly fast on his feet for a cripple who dragged his right leg. The glasses were filled to the brim, but he set them down on the table without spilling a drop. Although he had obviously been a waiter for some time, he seemed absurdly out of place among the soiled tablecloths, waxed-paper napkins, and potted palms with wilting fronds that stood about the room. With his straw-colored, untrimmed beard, his earlocks, the yarmulka on the bald crown of his head, he looked to Yigael as if he had wandered in here by mistake on his way to one of the dark, smelly synagogues in Mea Shearim.

"What's this?" Yigael asked him.

"What's it look like? It's your check."

"What's the rush?"

"You call yourself a Jew? Tonight's the beginning of Tisha b'Av."

"What is it?" asked Elana, who had been concentrating on her ice cream.

"Tisha b'Av," Yigael repeated, sipping his brandy.

"Is that so? Do you fast?" she asked the waiter, and explained to Yigael, "My grandfather always fasted on Tisha b'Av and slept with his head on a stone."

"In this country?"

"On the floor of his apartment on Herzl Street, in Tel Aviv."

"There's something peculiar about the whole thing," said Yigael.

"What do you mean?"

"Think about it for a moment. What's the literal meaning of Tisha b'Av?"

"The ninth day of the Hebrew month of Av," said Elana.

"Well, according to the Second Book of Kings, the Babylonians burned down Jerusalem and the temple on the seventh of Av, but Jeremiah says it happened on the tenth."

"So what?"

"Don't you see? Why fast on the ninth? It's the wrong day." He swirled the brandy in the snifter grasped in his hand. "The Talmud has some elaborate explanation, but I forget what it is." He swallowed the brandy. "There's some evidence that the ninth of Av was a Babylonian festival the Jews picked up during the exile there."

"What kind of festival?"

"Something to do with the death of Tammuz, I think—the god of fertility. In any case, the Jews apparently adapted it for their own purposes."

"Listen, mister, how about the check? It's almost sundown. I've got to go to shul," the waiter insisted. He spoke Hebrew with a strong Polish-Yiddish accent.

"Where're you from?" Yigael asked as he paid up.

"Here and there."

"Warsaw?"

"Yes, Warsaw, too," the waiter said. "Why?"

"My father came from Warsaw."

"Oh?" The waiter stopped fumbling in his pocket for the change and looked at Yigael with interest for the first time. "Was he there during the war?"

"No, he came here in 1932."

"Lucky."

"Not at all," said Yigael. "Smart. He was a Zionist."

"And his family?"

"They stayed in Warsaw and were killed during the war."

"In the ghetto?"

"In Auschwitz."

"What was their name?"

"Janower."

"I knew a Rabbi Lazer Janower in Auschwitz," the waiter said. "A great Talmudic scholar. But he was from Vilna. Any relation?"

"Not that I know," said Yigael, unable to keep the contempt out of his voice. He had met this type before—the kind who had undoubtedly been deported without protest, who, at night in the barracks, had never failed to gratefully mumble the blessing over a crust of moldy bread. His yellowish, bloodshot eyes had seen in the heaps of naked corpses the will of God.

"That's O.K. Forget it. Keep the change," Yigael said, waving him away in disgust.

The man shambled off, the tray under one arm, dragging his right foot. His rubber heel left a black streak on the tiles between the wilting potted palms. Elana was again licking her spoon with the greediness of a child. Yigael closed his eyes. The double brandy had gone right to his head and made him sweat. It was too damn hot to drink. Jerusalem was having a particularly hot summer, and now, to top it off, the newspapers were predicting a khamsin. Maybe it had already begun. The restaurant was stifling. There was the smell of burned fat in the air. Had there been a fire in the kitchen?

"Do you smell something burning?" he asked Elana. She shook her head, and, sure enough, when Yigael sniffed the air again he detected nothing. It was a trick of the mind, he realized. The brandy stinging his tongue, the heat, the sweat trickling down between his shoulder blades had evoked the smell of fatty sausages frying in a pan over a portable gas stove. He was with his reserve unit again, on the canal, opposite Ismailia, in an underground bunker where the sausages sizzled and a bottle of Rémy Martin was being passed from hand to hand. It was a celebration. For almost twenty minutes now, there had been a lull in the Egyptian barrage, which had begun at dawn, four hours before. The bottle was passed to him again. There was one good swallow left. He decided to save it for Uri, who was in command of a communications bunker a kilometer up the line.

And then standing on the steps was the red-headed medic from Haifa, who in the last week had developed a twitch in his left eyelid.

"Yigael, it's Uri. You'd better come."

"What happened?"

"A fluke," the medic said. "One of those things. He was in the slit trench, on his way back from the latrine, when the attack started."

"Is he dead?"

The eyelid twitched. "The first shell. A one-twenty-two from a howitzer."

The lid twitched again, and he added plaintively, "We did all we could. We found all of him except the right arm below the elbow."

The waiter re-emerged from the kitchen and began to scrape and clack his way on the tiles across the room; he had replaced his shoes with wooden-soled slippers. Elana eyed him curiously over the glass of water raised to her lips and said, "My grandfather used to wear those things to go to synagogue on Tisha b'Av, too. Why do religious Jews take off their shoes when they mourn?"

"What's the difference?"

"It makes no sense to me."

"Tisha b'Av makes no sense," said Yigael. "Not anymore. There's no need for it anymore." And he watched the man leave the restaurant through the glass door and turn down Jaffa Road. The door remained ajar; for a moment after the man was out of sight, the scrape and clack of his wooden soles still grated on Yigael's ears: an echo from the past—like the man himself, who was limping off to mourn the destruction of a city that had been rebuilt and an exile that had finally been brought to an end.

"It's easy to see why you and Uri were so close," Elana said.

"We grew up together."

"It's much more than that. He didn't read poetry as a rule, but he was always quoting . . . Is it Shlonsky?"

Yigael's attention had momentarily strayed back to the glass door. The setting sun flashed on a window above the pharmacy across the street; a scrap of paper fluttered against the curb. Then the verse she was reciting caught at him:

> There is no angel there.
> The boy must free himself
> And seize the knife,
> Bind up his father,
> Throw the altar down.
>
> There is no Covenant.
> The sacrifice we make
> Is for a portion promised us
> By no one but ourselves.

"No, it's not Shlonsky," said Yigael. "I can't remember who wrote it. Maybe Lamdan."

"It makes no difference. It meant a great deal to him. It was the only poem he knew by heart." She smiled dimly. "He taught it to me one night last winter when he was drunk. But you know something?" she added. "For the life of me, I can't remember the sound of his voice. Can you imagine that? He's only been dead six weeks."

"That's perfectly natural."

"Is it really? I didn't know."

He stared at her in amazement, and with envy. After all, she was twenty-three. She had been born here, had lived through three wars, but up till now had somehow managed to escape unscathed. He resented her luck. At her age, he had already buried his father and at least three good friends. His father had been killed in the fight for Jish, up north, in 1948. All that remained of him in Yigael's memory were his bushy mustache, prematurely streaked with gray, and a pair of round, steel-rimmed glasses.

He rose unsteadily to his feet. "Come on," he said. "You must be tired. I'll take you home."

As they crossed the Street of the Prophets, a dry, hot wind, laden with dust, blew in their faces—the khamsin, at last, from the Wilderness of Judea, carrying with it a faint odor of scorched wild flowers and withered grass. The particles of dust streamed in the headlights of a passing car. Yigael coughed; the girl stumbled and clutched at his arm. A strand of her hair, which brushed his cheek, was already damp and tangled with sweat.

They continued up Strauss Street. At the entrance to the hospital, a Home Guard, with a Lee-Enfield slung awkwardly over one shoulder, sucked furiously on his unlit pipe. He had wrinkled lips, white eyebrows. Ten years too old for the active reserve, he had been called up, thought Yigael, to protect those only a little more defenseless than himself.

There was a small synagogue on the next corner. Yigael glanced through an open window on the ground floor. Elana, who lived up the block, tugged at his sleeve, but the sight held him: the Ark and the *bimah* draped in black cloth, the overturned benches, the fifteen or twenty men seated in a dim circle of light on the stone floor. Their shadows wavered on the wall. All the lights in the place had been extinguished, Yigael realized, except for the brass oil lamp suspended from the ceiling on a chain before the Ark. The wick smoked.

Elana pulled again at his sleeve. "In a minute," said Yigael. An old man on the *bimah* was chanting from the Book of Lamentations in a nasal voice: " 'Jerusalem remembereth in the days of her affliction and her anguish all her treasures that she had in the days of old. . . .' "

"I've got to get home," said Elana. "I've got to take a shower. I'm all in." The urgency of her tone made Yigael look at her. Her face was streaming with sweat. "It's the damn khamsin," she explained. "It always gets on my nerves. Uri once told me that when the Turks were here their judges were very lenient with people who committed crimes during a khamsin." She ran her fingers through her stringy hair and rambled on, "He was thinking of doing a book on the administration of Ottoman law in Palestine—did you know that? It interested him very much. He had already done some of the research. I have his notes."

The wind had dropped a little; the nasal chant in the synagogue rose.

"We lived together almost six months," said Elana. "I gave away all his clothes. One loose-leaf notebook and a few of his letters are all I have left."

"You'll have the child," said Yigael.

"Yes. I'm counting on that." Her face still shone with sweat, but she seemed calmer, as if her anxiety had diminished with the wind. "By the way, the wedding is at three. My parents have hired a car. We can pick you up at the university, if you like."

"That'd be fine," Yigael said. "What about the ring?"

"All taken care of. I bought one last week in a little shop on Ben Yehuda. Fourteen-karat gold, and wide—I like wide wedding bands—but very reasonable."

A wide gold band. It was something Yigael could easily visualize, and with it he pictured a wineglass wrapped in a white handkerchief, and, for some reason, a fringed chuppah, embroidered with roses, casting its shadow on the grave.

"Did you invite Levi?" he asked.

"Will he be out of the hospital?"

"No, but he'd appreciate an invitation."

"I'll write him tomorrow."

On the *bimah*, the old man blew his nose into his fingers, and, as Yigael turned away, resumed his nasal chant: " 'Zion spreadeth forth her hands, and there is none to comfort her. . . .' "

"We'll pick you up at two in front of the library," said Elana. "Is that O.K.?"

"Yes," Yigael said, but his voice broke, and he averted his face, astonished by the tears that welled up in his eyes.

UNDER SIEGE: A JOURNAL

24 June 1974

Aliza Wolfe suspects that two couples from Tel Aviv who sent regrets are scared to come up here next Tuesday for her daughter Ruthie's wedding. She's worried that more will do the same.

At 7 P.M., along with her husband Shlomo, we go to the dining hall for supper. I count nine men with automatic weapons: Kalashnikovs, Carl Gustavs, and Uzis. The loaded magazines are on the tables beside plastic dishes filled with chopped cucumbers, carrots, boiled potatoes, and sour cream. Shlomo tells me that twenty men have been issued guns from the arsenal, with orders to carry them at all times.

"It's been like this for a couple of weeks now," he says. "Ever since Shamir."

He's referring to the terrorist attack on Kibbutz Shamir, ten kilometers to the southeast, in which two women were murdered on 13 June.

"The terrorists were going for the children when two of them were shot," he says. "The other two were trapped near the barn for about fifteen minutes. They exchanged fire with the kibbutz members until the corpses blew up."

"The corpses?"

He butters a piece of bread. "Just like that—bang!—on the path, followed a minute or two later by the two who were still alive in the bee house. They all exploded."

"I don't understand."

"They're walking bombs. They have explosives strapped to them which are detonated by remote control."

He chews on the bread. Tojo, the military commander of the kibbutz, comes over to say hello. He packs a Luger in a canvas holster on his hip. He and Mark, who's American, will guard the children's houses tonight.

9:30 P.M.

With Edith and Seymour on the porch outside their room. Seymour is in pain. The stump of his right leg has never healed. Nine years ago, his leg was blown off above the knee by a land mine planted by infiltrators on the road to the orchard. He has an appointment next week for an examination at Tel Hashomer Hospital near Tel Aviv. Edith, a registered nurse, thinks the oozing stump must be operated on.

The sounds of six explosions in the west. Edith believes Kiriat Shemona is being hit again by Katyusha rockets. Three orange parachute flares burn for five minutes in the southern sky.

26 June 1974

Last night, terrorists murdered a mother and her two children in Naharia, about sixty kilometers west of here. Aliza tells me what happened two months ago in Kiriat Shemona.

"It was on a Thursday. Just after breakfast. About eight o'clock, I was putting laundry away in the children's house when I heard a loud thuds—explosions—and a siren going off in the distance. I rushed out and looked in the direction of Kiriat Shemona. There was black smoke—clouds of it—boiling up above the town. Then there were three more explosions, one right after another, and I ran down to the dining hall where Amnon, the kibbutz secretary, said that the terrorists were making an attack. They murdered eighteen people before our soldiers killed them.

"We watched the battle from the lawn. You could see lots of black smoke and hear explosions. It was a beautiful spring day. When the wind was right, you could smell the wild hyacinths in the fields. Then, at twelve o'clock, there was a terrific blast, and silence.

"Shlomo drove five of us into Kiriat Shemona. Yehuda Halevi Street was covered with broken glass. There was barbed wire everywhere, lots of soldiers and police. The crowd was in a frenzy. I saw one old woman scratch her cheeks with her fingernails. The man next to her was frothing at the mouth.

"I stood opposite the house where it happened. The front was blown away. Two walls were missing. I could see everything inside. There was a television set, on the second floor, in a sink. In the corner, I saw a man pulling on a naked leg. It belonged to a terrorist's corpse. The crowd screamed, 'Throw down the corpse! Throw down the corpse!' I shut my eyes. The roar made me look. I saw a jerrican of petrol being passed from hand to hand. A kid in front of me jumped up and down. Another doused the corpse with the petrol. The crowd roared again. I can still smell the burning flesh."

There's always a guard, armed with an Uzi, seated on a folding chair in front of the house where the infants and young children live. This one, in his early forties, has an unfamiliar face: long sideburns, a gold tooth, dark skin. He is one of the soldiers doing their stint in the reserve here. During the day another guard is at the only gate in the eight-foot-high fence, topped by barbed wire and mercury-vapor lamps, which completely surrounds the kibbutz. At night, from dusk till dawn, six more are on duty in the steel watchtowers, mounted with machine guns. They overlook the Lebanese frontier, which is about a third of a mile due north of here. Shlomo says, "We haven't got enough men for the job."

At age forty-seven, he must stand guard for eight hours once every ten days—after working an eight-hour shift in the kibbutz factory, where he maintains the machinery. This is in addition to serving thirty days a year as a demolitions expert in the army reserve. He's been fighting one war since 1947, when he was in the Palmach. We walk back to his room. He bounces along on the balls of his feet, toes turned out. Once he stops, bends down, and moves a child's rusty tricycle off the path. The seat, which is askew, attracts his attention, and he sets it right, tightening the bolt with his callused fingers.

Their eighteen-year-old son, Adi, is spending a year with the kibbutz youth movement working with new immigrants who have been settled in Ma'alot. He was in a building next to the school which was attacked by terrorists on May 15.

Midnight

In bed for the last half hour reading Aliza's copy of *The Viking Portable Oscar Wilde. The Picture of Dorian Gray* doesn't hold up.

27 June 1974

Everyone is convinced there'll be another war with the Arabs; their aim is the annihilation of the Jewish state.

Zvi says, "Listen! My grandfather fought the Arabs and so will my grandchildren."

At 4 P.M., over cheesecake and iced coffee, Aliza mentions the concentration camp in which her parents were murdered: Salas Pils, near Riga. "The prisoners all starved to death." In 1939, at the age of eight, Aliza was sent by her parents from Germany to England. She was adopted by a Jewish family in Leeds. In 1946 she found out her parents were dead. She became a Zionist. Two years later, she came to Israel and joined the kibbutz.

She says, "My father was a butcher. I have a memory of him being forced by the Gestapo to dig a grave."

28 June 1974

"He's a pain in the ass!"

This, in her thick Chicago accent from Edith, about Chick, who follows us into the dining hall at lunch. His left leg below the knee is in a steel brace, and he leans to the right on a cane as he lurches through the swinging doors.

While fighting in the Sinai during the October war he was hit by a piece of shrapnel that broke his pelvis, paralyzed his leg, and came out through his stomach. Five and a half meters of intestine were removed. The wound has been closed for almost two months, but he remains depressed and filled with self-pity.

She says, "It's about time he got a grip on himself."

8 P.M.

With Harry, in his room. In a voice hoarse from chain-smoking, he reminisces about the founding of the kibbutz in 1947.

"The land belonged to six Arab families—very rich—who lived in Lebanon, and was in the process of being bought up by the

Jewish National Fund. When we were advised to come here and settle, two hundred dunums had already been bought and negotiations were going on for the rest. The people who lived in the Arab village here were tenant farmers who worked for those six families. Before we could get full possession of the land, we had to negotiate with them, too. In other words, we had to pay for the land twice, which sometimes almost doubled the price. But slowly and surely, we bought it up."

29 June 1974

David says, "Our greatest crisis is when our kids go into the army. They volunteer for the most responsible and dangerous jobs —it's become a tradition for kids from kibbutzim—but we can't complain. After all, we fed them with stories all their lives of what we did when we were in the Palmach."

David's twenty-one-year-old son, Yuval, is a commando. Ofer, Harry's boy, is an underwater demolition expert. Leb's son, Guy, flies a Skyhawk. Adi has just been asked to apply for a top-secret outfit, the nature of which he's not allowed to discuss. None of them will talk to me about his army service. At lunch, I try to pump Ofer; he grins.

Chava, whose son, Gidi, is a radar installation officer in the air force, says, "They don't talk about their feelings. Sometimes they joke about them.

"During the last war, the radio broadcast birth announcements to the front. If it was a girl, the men would say to the father, 'Mazel tov, you have a widow!' If it was a boy, 'Mazel tov! A casualty!' "

10:20 P.M.

In the turret of Watchtower 5, writing by the light of an electric lantern. Shlomo sits to my right, less than a foot away, on another steel chair bolted to the steel floor, behind a 7.92-mm German machine gun. The muzzle sticks out of the window, from which the double pane has been removed.

The mercury-vapor lamps light up the fence. Beyond, a dark field. And beyond that, some 700 meters to the northeast, is the Lebanese frontier. We've been sitting here now since ten, when we relieved the first watch of the night, and will remain until six tomorrow morning. My ass hurts.

Shlomo loads the machine gun with a belt of fifty cartridges, in a basket magazine, then says, "Now all you have to do is take it off safety and pull this handle back as far as it will go."

He also has two grenades, which he keeps on the floor next to his right foot. And on his hip, in a canvas holster, he carries a .22-caliber Beretta pistol; an extra clip, wrapped in plastic, is stuck in the breast pocket of his shirt.

10:45 P.M.

The turret, on ball bearings, revolves at the touch of a hand. Mounted on top is a searchlight aligned with the gun. Shlomo turns us slowly to the right, then stops—there's a brake under his foot—and switches on the light. It shines on a eucalyptus tree about 300 meters away.

11 P.M.

Every fifteen minutes another guard in a Volkswagen truck without lights passes beneath us on the new asphalt road that runs on this side of the fence around the kibbutz.

2:20 A.M.

The sounds of machine-gun and artillery fire in the dark to the northeast.

30 June 1974

Aliza is no longer worried that the situation here will keep any other guests from coming to the wedding. She's worried about everything else: whether the rabbi from Kiriat Shemona will show up in time; how to keep the flies off the food being served outdoors; the length of her dress.

1 July 1974

Ruthie and her fiancé, Deddie, have arrived from Jerusalem, where they have been living together for almost a year. They squabble all afternoon. Just before supper, in the middle of another argument, Deddie throws his arms around her neck and kisses her on the mouth. He's a handsome boy of twenty-six, with a degree from the Hebrew University, and is the assistant to the Director General of the Ministry of Education.

In the evening, we visit on the porch and chat. He is proud of being a "left Zionist" who disagrees with Dayan's policy toward the Arabs in the Occupied Territories.

"It's criminal," he says.

"What do you suggest instead?"

"Let them establish a Palestinian state." He adds, "But without one soldier or one gun."

He goes inside to be with Ruthie, who's ironing her bridal veil. The leaves rustle. Five minutes later, he pokes his head out of the screen door and says,

"Look. No one in this country wanted to be unjust to the Arabs. But we were. We had to be in order to get justice for ourselves. Now it's our justice against theirs. I prefer ours."

2 July 1974

After the outdoor ceremony, under the faded chuppah and colored lights, I overhear Aliza talking with Shlomo's sister-in-law.

"I haven't seen it yet myself, but Ruthie says it's marvelous— four big rooms on the ground floor with a garden that has a view of the Valley of Kidron and the walls of the Old City."

"But that's in the Arab part of town."

"Yes, I know. That's why it's so cheap."

"How much?"

"Four hundred pounds a month."

"It's a steal."

Aliza: "I hope it's safe."

9 P.M.

Edith tells me that the doctors at Tel Hashomer have diagnosed Seymour's trouble as chronic dermatitis, an inflammation of the skin on his stump.

She invites me to their room, where he is watching a TV show about some of the men who commanded the tubs on which illegal immigrants were smuggled into the country in 1947. He knows them all. Over a Scotch, he talks about his own experiences as a twenty-year-old American volunteer on those leaky tubs spattered with bloody vomit from the seasick passengers. Aliza and Shlomo join us. We gossip about the wedding guests. Deddie doesn't get along with his father, who's a big shot in the Likud.

6 July 1974

Aliza is concerned about Yaakov's eight-year-old boy, who's name is Dov. Yaakov was one of the three kibbutz members killed in the Six Day War. Dov dresses up in girl's clothes.

Chava says through the screen door, "Mark was shot in the orchard by terrorists."

Aliza says, "Let's get the kids to the shelters."

Outside the children's house we run into Edith, who says, "False alarm. Mark shot himself in the right elbow while cleaning his AK-47. He was rushed to the hospital in Safed."

1 A.M.

In bed. A distant burst of machine-gun fire. Leafing through Aliza's paperback copy of *The Magic Mountain,* I discover two sentences underlined with a ballpoint pen:

> I will keep faith with death in my heart, yet well remember that
> faith with death and the dead is evil, is hostile to humankind, so
> soon as we give it power over thought and action. For the sake of
> goodness and love, man shall let death have no sovereignty over
> his thoughts.

EXILE:
A JOURNAL

27 December 1985

Dear Hugh,

  Hope that this arrives before you leave for L.A. Adi's address is 1794 Martel Ave. L.A. 90046. Tel: (213) 851-4476. How I hope you meet and have a chance to talk. Shlomo and I can't figure out what's been keeping him in the States. It's been almost four years! When we ask we don't get satisfactory answers. I want to know what you think. We worry so. It seems to us that he's living from day to day without any thought for the future. He'll soon be thirty-one, for God's sake! Anyway, please let me know.

  The Lebanese border is again tense. Yesterday we were warned that the Shiites might attack us with Katyusha at any time. Spent today cleaning out the shelters. I knew in my heart that our invasion of Lebanon was useless. Does Adi ever open up about his experiences there? He never mentions them to us.

  We send you, Marilyn, Kate, and Kore all our love. Enjoy your trip to L.A. I hope you sell your book to the movies! Please, please write after you see Adi.

      All the best,
      Aliza

18 January 1986
Saturday
10:30 A.M.

  In the back yard of 1794 Martel Avenue, Los Angeles, after two drags of Adi's hash. He brought half an ounce from New York, where he partied from Christmas Eve to New Year's Day with a redhead named Sue. "She's fantastic! A Mormon. Beautiful blue eyes! Maybe I'll marry her."

Barefoot, he wears white swimming trunks, no shirt. The scars from the bullet wounds on his left shoulder, above the armpit, and the front of his left thigh are about an inch long and half an inch wide.

He picks up the phone on the table and calls; no answer. "Her name is Natalie. She's a Jesus freak who lives in San Diego. I'd like to marry her too."

Out comes a jar of pickles he preserved with capers. "Best you ever ate," he says.

We talk a bit about his father, who assembles plastic irrigation sprinklers in the kibbutz factory.

Adi: "He's gonna be sixty years old. He hates his job, but that's where the kibbutz needs him. His religion is Labor Zionism: the kibbutz, Israel—a better future for the Jews. That's all he lived for since the age of seventeen: a better future. When's that? The future never comes. I want to be happy now."

Another drag each from the corncob pipe; I gobble up the last pickle. Adi puts down a plate of green olives. The warm sun, stucco bungalow, ripe oranges on the tree beside the wooden shack, make me think of Tel Aviv. In fact, on the other side of the garden fence, two women are chatting in Hebrew. Adi says the neighborhood is filled with Israelis, blacks, and gays.

He then says, "I got my green card. I'm a legal resident. I'm going to become an American citizen. This is the only country where you can live your own life. But if there's a war with Russia, I won't fight. I'll never kill again. I'm a pacifist. I'll go to Mexico on my bike."

His Yamaha 750 is parked in the driveway. No more green olives. We polish off a pint of coffee ice cream, and he asks, "Are you happy?"

"Very."

"Then I'm happy too."

He lights a Marlboro from the one burning between his fingers; the ground is littered with filtered butts.

He says, "I like working with my hands. That's the great thing about this country. If you've got good hands, you'll never go hungry. I work when I feel like it. I never have trouble getting a job because I got a great—how do you say?—reputation with Israelis here as a hard worker. Last couple of months, I've been installing solar heating panels for two guys who got a business on Fairfax Avenue—that's the Israeli ghetto in L.A. The money is very good. Five hundred dollars a week.

"I live in the wood shack. Four Mexicans lived there before me. My rent is two hundred dollars a month for one room with a toilet, a shower, and an electric heater. I cook out here on the grill or in the kitchen I share with another Israeli guy named Yoav, who owns the house. He's been in the States twelve years. He's a partner in two laundromats on Fairfax. There are two hundred thousand of us Israelis in L.A., and doing very well. We're smart and tough."

He grinds out the Marlboro beneath his naked heel—a trick of his father's—and says, "I'm saving up to visit my parents in April."

"They'll appreciate it."

"The first time my father visited me in the hospital after I was wounded, his face was white. I never saw him so pale. He looked like he was gonna have a heart attack. I got scared."

Enter Yoav, who relights the pipe, takes a drag, and passes it around the table.

11:30 A.M.
  Like Adi, Yoav is an ex-kibbutznik, born and bred at Ma-ayan Zvi, outside Haifa. Forty; blue eyes, thin, sandy hair, muscles. He tells me that his two brothers are dead; one was killed at Latrun during the War of Independence and the other on the Golan in 1967. "My younger brother's death finished my mother off in six months. My father lasted till the spring. This was a guy who came to Israel from Berlin in 1923. He was a pioneer in the country; one of the founders of the kibbutz. An idealist! Before he died, he said to me, 'My life was a mistake. I should have gone to the United States like my sister Ruth.'

"I was in a MASH unit on the Canal, in '73. It freaked me out. I spent a year on an ashram in India. My guru was a Burmese Buddhist named Goenka. He taught me the Vipashina way to meditate. I got my head together, then came here. My father's sister helped me get my green card. I became an American citizen on January 19, 1979—the biggest day of my life."

Adi says, "My mother comes also from Germany. Her parents and brother were killed in the Holocaust. She was sent alone to England at age eight. Israel has been her home since 1949. The country is her life. Same with my father, who was born in Safed. He wanted to be an architect; instead he joined Palmach—the Yiftach Brigade—and fought in the War of Independence. Then he joined the kibbutz. Zionism! Socialism! Duty to others! I'm finished with that! Ever read *Atlas Shrugged,* by Ayn Rand? Her philosophy I like: Freedom! Your duty is to yourself!"

Yoav says, "Israel is the new Chelm."

We sit in the sun. Yoav, chain-smoking Camels, reads the weekly Hebrew tabloid *Israel Shelanu* ("Our Israel"), published in New York for ex-Israelis. Photos of Sharon, Topol, the Lubavitcher rebbe, Helena Rubinstein, Arafat, Mengele.

Adi, on the phone to a travel agent, makes a deal for a week's vacation, beginning next Wednesday, in Hawaii. "Not bad. Five hundred forty bucks, round trip, including a hotel room in Maui, for six nights, plus a car."

I asked Yoav, "Why do you call Israel the new Chelm?"

"Chelm is the city of fools."

"I know what Chelm is."

"You know why it's a city of fools?"

"No."

"Because everybody there is Jewish. Nobody in his right mind wants to live only among Jews."

Adi phones a girl named Shoshana and in a mixture of Hebrew and English asks her to go with him to Maui next Wednesday. "No? Are you sure? If you come with me, I'll marry you."

Noon

Adi: "My outfit took Ein Hilweh, a Palestinian refugee camp in Sidon. We fought there a week. House to house, block to block. The place was crowded with civilians; lots of kids and old people. The PLO fighters wouldn't let anybody surrender. They fought to the death, Ein Hilweh is their Masada, their Warsaw Ghetto. We brought in planes and heavy artillery. The ground shook, the sky was filled with black smoke for days. What a stink!

Napalm, gunpowder, corpses, open sewers. You couldn't tell who the enemy was. An old man blew up Guni Simcha, my radioman, with a hand grenade. I learned fast to shoot first. Early Sunday morning—the sixth day—a fourteen- or fifteen-year-old-kid stuck his head out of a doorway in an alley near the school and I shot him between the eyes. Then I searched his body for weapons. There were none. I made up my mind, 'Never again! I won't kill again.' "

Yoav (leaving): "Israel sucks."

Adi asks me, "You eat pork?"

"Yes, of course."

"Good, I'll grill us pork chops for lunch. I love cooking. I planted that mint over there and oregano, also onions and carrots in the garden. The smell of oregano reminds me of the kibbutz."

2 P.M.

We put away four grilled chops apiece and two bottles of Beaujolais. Adi picks his front teeth with a folded matchbook—like his father—and says,

"After Sidon, I fought in West Beirut, but didn't kill anybody. At the end of August, I got a forty-eight-hour leave and headed home. As I was walking up the road to the kibbutz I saw a guy in the orchard, under an apple tree, about one hundred yards off to my right. A stranger, wearing a double-breasted jacket and jeans. He looked like an Arab. I put the clip back in my M-16 and went over to check him out.

"I said, 'What are you doing here?'

"He says to me—in good Hebrew, but with an Arab accent— 'I'm a guard. The kibbutz hired me to guard the orange trees.'

"I told him, 'Orange trees? What orange trees? Orange trees don't grow in the Galilee.'

"He reached inside his buttoned jacket, whipped out a 9-mm pistol—probably from his belt—and shot me in the shoulder and thigh. We were, say, four feet apart. I heard two loud bangs but saw one flash of light. I felt no pain; only something like two terrific electric shocks, one after the other, up front, in my left side. I took one step back, with my left foot, and at the same time squeezed off a long burst. The bullets tore open his chest. The next thing I remember is looking down at his face. He was about my age. His eyes were open. His skin turned dirty yellow from loss of blood. I was bleeding all over the place myself."

"Did you pass out?"

"No. Not once the whole time. I'm very strong. Lucky, too. I made it back to the road. A few minutes later, I got picked up by the four o'clock bus from the kibbutz to Kiriat Shemona and rushed to town. A medic there knocked me out with a shot. I liked that a lot. Next morning I woke up in the hospital at Safed. My parents were there; also a cop. He told me I killed a Yemenite Jew from Kiriat Shemona named Bobby Zachari. He was a half-wit; maybe a little crazy. A gun runner and dope smuggler. His gang smuggled stolen Israeli guns—Uzis, Galil assault rifles—into Lebanon and brought back hashish."

3:30 P.M.

I meet my pal Bob Avrech on the parking lot. He wears a beard and yarmulka. He says, "No sale. I can't get any producer interested in making a movie from your book."

"Thanks anyway."

"I'd like to have done the screenplay."

"You'd have done a good job."

Avrech wrote *Body Double* for Brian DePalma. We stroll east on Sunset, passed the Professional Waiters' School ("We train you to work in elegant restaurants"); there is nobody else on the sidewalk, east or west, for blocks and blocks.

He says, "At my yeshiva—I studied at the Yeshiva of Flatbush, on Coney Island Avenue—Talmud bored me. The book of Esther turned me on. King Ahasuerus gets drunk at the feast and commands his wife to dance naked in front of his guests; she refuses and he kills her. Wow!"

We stop at the restaurant on the corner of Sunset and Poinsettia for a cup of coffee. Avrech opens the glass door, takes one sniff, and backs out, saying, "The smell of bacon turns my stomach."

On the next block, he says, "Karen and I moved out here from Brooklyn about a year ago. L.A. is where the action is for a screenwriter. I'm doing very well. We bought a house in a Jewish neighborhood—Pico-Robertson. There's a good yeshiva for our kids, lots of kosher stores and shuls. It's like living in Israel. Even the light is the same. Have you noticed?"

"Would you live in Israel?"

"No. My work is here. Besides, America's my home. I never questioned that. Leastways, not till a week ago Thursday."

"What happened then?"

"My cousin Sam called me about two A.M. from Iowa City. He was an intern at a big hospital there, I forget which. We grew up together in Flatbush and went to the same yeshiva; he wears a beard and yarmulka, too. Our beards make us look a lot alike. Anyway, late Wednesday night the ambulance brings a farmer into the emergency room with a broken leg. Sam goes to help him.

"The farmer takes one look and says, 'You a Jew?'

"Sam says, 'Yeah.'

"The guy pulls out a pistol and says, 'Don't touch me. I'll kill you. You Jews stole my farm.' "

"What'd Sam do?"

"Left the guy on the table, cleaned out his locker, went home, and called me. He's been offered a job in a hospital in Milwaukee and will probably take it. There's a big Jewish community in Milwaukee."

An hour later

Driving to Malibu in my rented Toyota, Adi and I get stuck on Santa Monica Boulevard behind a station wagon. Its bumper sticker says, "Don't postpone joy!"

Adi asks, "What's 'postpone' mean?"

" 'Put off. Delay.' "

"That's good," he says. "Really good. 'Don't postpone joy!' That's what I believe."

"Me too."

THE PIT:

A JOURNAL

2 April 1986

With Marilyn today at the village of Izieu, about 50 miles east of Lyon. We found the big white farmhouse from which forty-four Jewish kids and seven Jewish adults were deported to Auschwitz in 1944—forty-two years ago this Sunday.

The house is owned by an old couple named Thibaudier. Marilyn translated what Mme. Thibaudier said. She planted begonias in the pot below the plaque on the wall which commemorates the dead. The pansies put there by Mme. Zlatin don't do well in the cold. Mme. Zlatin lives in Paris, but often comes to Izieu. She'll be here Sunday for the anniversary of the roundup (la rafle). Mme. Zlatin and her husband were in charge of the houseful of children during the war. She was in the South, at Montpellier, the day the Germans came; M. Zlatin was shot in a German prison camp.

5 April 1986

Spent two hours this morning with Cynthia Haft in her office at Yad Vashem, the Israeli memorial to the Holocaust. Cynthia is five months pregnant. Her office is on the first floor of the Research Center: a big building, next to the Hall of Remembrance, made from rosy blocks of Jerusalem stone. She does PR for Yad Vashem and is the Israeli representative of the Sons and Daughters of the Deported Jews of France.

I got her name from Serge Klarsfeld's book, *The Children of Izieu: A Human Tragedy.* * "I need your help. I've been to Izieu.

---

*New York: Harry N. Abrams, 1985.

I'm Jewish. I want to write about one of those forty-four kids. One I can identify with: a boy who'd now be about my age, if he'd lived. I need information about him. Details of his life. Would you have anything like that in your archives? Can you suggest a boy for me to write about?"

She said, "Georgy Halpern. He's the one for you. I'll give you letters he wrote to his parents from the house at Izieu. They live in Jerusalem, but they won't see you. They refused Beate Klarsfeld, who came with French TV. They won't talk with anybody about Georgy."

I looked up Georgy in Klarsfeld's book, which is a compilation of documents about the dead children. He was born 30 October 1935, in Vienna. His mother was separated from him—her only child—because she was sick. She was in a sanatorium near Izieu when Georgy was picked up.

I found him in the photo on the book's cover, taken at Izieu in the summer of 1943. He's fourth from the left, up front, the kid sitting on the grass, with bare feet, who grins at the camera.

At noon, I forced myself inside the Hall of Remembrance. "Join the army and travel the world, meet lots of interesting people and kill them." The slogan in English is printed in red letters across the back of a T-shirt worn by a fifteen-year-old Israeli boy; he's looking at the marble slab under which the ashes of murdered Jews are buried.

New York
16 July 1986

My daughter Kate is sixteen today. Theodor Reis was that age when he was taken at Izieu.

13 August 1986

Forty-three years ago today, Georgy wrote his mother from Izieu:

> The house is very pretty. Every Sunday we go to the Rhone and see the fishermen fish. There are big mountains. The village is very pretty. There are a lot of flowers, and trees and farms.

29 August 1986
Dear Mr. Nissenson,

Your letter & request to see us is a surprise. I asked Dr. Haft
to tell people not to call.

The reason: we are unable to speak about Georgy without great
emotion & that is what we can ill afford. My husband is 81 & I am
79 years old. He suffers from a heart condition and I fear the
consequences to him of talking about Georgy.

But if you are in Jerusalem contact us by phone.

No.———. We shall see then.

Sincerely,
(Signed)   Seraphine Halpern

1 September 1986

Forty-three years ago today, Georgy wrote his mother from
Izieu:

Soon it will be your birthday and I will make you a beautiful
surprise. I almost know how to swim. When we go for a walk we
always pick flowers to make a bouquet for the bedroom.

23 September 1986

Mrs. Halpern is eighty years old today.

30 September 1986

Today my daughter Kore is nine years old, the same age as
Charles Welter, Senta Spiegel, and Egon Gamiel when they were
taken at Izieu.

Room 908, The Tel Aviv Hilton
19 October 1986
8:30 A.M.

Mrs. Halpern answers her phone in English: "Wait till I turn
down the telly." We talk fifteen minutes before she agrees to see
me at 3 P.M. the next day. She asks for my room number at the
Hilton "in case I change my mind." She switches to German with
her husband, who has just awakened from a nap, and tells me,
"Julius will under no circumstances be present at our interview."

20 October 1986

Seraphine Friedmann Halpern, born in 1906 in Vienna, where she married Julius and had one son named Georges. At the Anschluss, in 1938, she and her husband sent the boy to Zurich; they fled to Paris. "When the war came, we brought the boy back." A tear rolls down her right cheek. She and the boy lived in Paris; Mr. Halpern was with the French army at Amiens. She contracted TB and wound up in a sanatorium in Hauteville near Izieu, in the department of Ain, where she twice suffered pulmonary collapse.

"I didn't know where Julius and Georgy were." (Up to now, she has referred to him as "the boy.")

"I found out later that Julius was taken by the French to a labor camp at Coures for Jews and Communists. He gave Georgy to the OSE (pronounced "Ozay")—the Oeuvre de Secours aux Enfants—the Jewish Children's Welfare Organization, who put him first into their children's home at Mainsat, and then into the one at Campestre, and finally, during late summer of 1943, Izieu.

"Julius joined the Maquis in the camp; the French army officer in command was a sympathizer, so Julius wasn't deported. Being a dentist also helped. Julius got false papers. He was a courier for the Resistance, so he could move around some.

"He once went to Izieu and brought Georgy from the home to a hotel at Hauteville, near the sanatorium. We spent the whole day together. The leaves were turning. We had lunch on the terrace. The bread was stale. Georgy was proud; he'd grown half an inch since leaving Campestre. He worried about being short."

She blows her nose into a shredded Kleenex. At 4:05 P.M., Dr. Halpern shuffles in wearing slippers. Mrs. Halpern speaks to him of me in French—"He recently visited Izieu"—and leaves us alone.

Dr. Halpern says, "You know there was a chap who denounced the kids to the Gestapo. His name was Lucien Bourdon. He was tried by a French court in 1947. He lost the right to vote for five years.

"I joined the Maquis in 1942. The French government gives me a little pension, you know. The camp was called Neuvik d'Ussel. We cut wood and fetched water. Jews were deported from there to Auschwitz every week; I was one lucky dentist. Seraphine, the little chap, and I were separated between 1939 and '42. I can't concentrate."

Mrs. Halpern comes back in the room with a fresh box of Klee-nex. "After the war, Julius and I lived in Lyon, Paris, and finally Brighton, England, where Julius was a dentist for thirty years."

Dr. Halpern: "I got the news about the little chap in a letter written by the director of the sanatorium. She got it from the fishmonger who supplied the children at Izieu. He told her, 'The children were taken away Thursday.' She wrote me. I told Sera-phine May 8th—the day the war ended."

Mrs. Halpern (weeping): "Life is hell."

"I spent a day alone with the little chap at Izieu. He took my hand, and said, 'Papa, how will you find me after the war?' I can't get over that. He was safe in Zurich. I brought him to France so we could all be together. I feel guilty for his death. I'm ashamed to tell people how I lost my child."

25 October 1986

　　Today Klaus Barbie is seventy-three.

30 October 1986

　　Today Georgy would have been fifty-one.

11 November 1986

　　Forty-four years ago today, SS Obersturmführer Klaus Bar-bie set up his Gestapo headquarters in Lyon at the Hotel Ter-minus. He tortured people in a bathtub filled with water on the fifth floor. The naked prisoner was forced to crouch on the tiles. His wrists were tied to his ankles, and a pole was inserted through the crook of the elbows and behind the knees. The pole was laid across the width of the tub, suspending the prisoner over the water, into which he was plunged headfirst, again and again.

14 November 1986

　　Forty-three years ago today, Georgy wrote:

> In the morning we eat cocoa and bread and jam. At noon we have soup, salad, and apple. At 4, we have bread and jam, milk.

7 February 1987

> Forty-three years ago today, Georgy wrote:

> There is a big porch from which we see all the mountains which
> are covered with snow. I have no shorts and socks. The directoress
> says that you should send me 200 francs to buy shoes.

9 February 1987

> Forty-four years ago today in Lyon, Klaus Barbie com-
manded the Gestapo raid on the offices of the Jewish Welfare
Organization at 12 rue Ste.-Catherine. One Jew escaped. Eighty-
five others were murdered in Auschwitz.

> On 28 February 1944 Georgy wrote:

> All the snow has melted. Now it is very sunny and we take walks
> on Sunday and Thursday.... We write penmanship, sums, science,
> geography.

From Georgy's undated letter to his father, written a few days
after the above:

> I would like to leave here because the children are nasty. They
> hurt me. They destroy my toys.

10 March 1987

> I'm fifty-four today.

6 April 1987

> Forty-three years ago today, Georgy and the others were
rounded up at Izieu. One adult—Leon Reifmann—escaped by
jumping from a window. The others, including a woman named
Lea Feldblum, were taken with the children to Lyon, where they
were jailed for a week in Fort Montluc.

> That evening, Barbie telexed the German Commander of the
Security Police for France:

> This morning the Jewish children's home in Izieu was cleaned
> out.

7 April 1987

> Forty-three years ago today, Georgy and the others were
transferred by train to the transit camp at Drancy. On 13 April,

Georgy and thirty-two other children and four adults from Izieu were deported to Auschwitz in a sealed boxcar.

15 April 1987

Forty-three years ago today, Georgy and the above arrived at the Birkenau station, Auschwitz. The same night, Georgy and the other children were killed.

1 May 1987

Seven years ago today, Barbie's son, Klaus-Georg, thirty-four, fell to his death in front of his father while hang-gliding in the Andes.

Cynthia Haft gave birth last August to a healthy girl. Her name is Caryana.

Dr. and Mrs. Halpern are O.K. Although associate plaintiffs against Barbie, they want nothing to do with the trial.

I learned the above today in New York from Beate Klarsfeld. She was born in Berlin in 1939. Protestant. Her father, who was not a member of the Nazi party, served in the Wehrmacht. Beate and her husband Serge are world-famous Nazi hunters. They uncovered Barbie's telex about the children, and Beate went to Bolivia, where she secured his extradition to France.

"What makes you care so much?"

"I'm ashamed of being German," she said. "I want to help my country regain its honor."

In 1960 she met Serge, whom she sometimes calls "Sasha."

"Sasha taught me about the Holocaust. I'd learned nothing about it from my mother and father. They never mentioned it while I was growing up. My husband educated me."

Serge, a French Jew, was hidden during the war in another children's home run by OSE. His father, Arno, fought in the French army; in 1943, he was arrested in Nice and deported to Auschwitz.

"After the war, Sasha spoke with a friend who knew Arno Klarsfeld in the camp. The friend remembered him as a big man with broad shoulders and strong arms who might have survived. But he attacked a kapo, who was beating another prisoner. The Germans sentenced him to dig coal at Furstengrubb—the slave labor camp near Auschwitz. He was worked to exhaustion, then gassed in August 1944.

"Arno Klarsfeld fought evil even though he had no hope. Can we do less? My parents were at first shocked by my behavior. What would the neighbors say? Mother didn't speak with me a long time. She's come round. Now she tells the neighbors, 'Did you see Beate on TV?'

"My mother-in-law and I got along from the start. She didn't care I'm German. She was a Jewish mama. She thought I'd make Sasha a good wife. She said, 'That's all that counts!' She and my mother eventually became close friends. They spoke German together. Mama was heartbroken when my mother-in-law died."

Q: "You and Mr. Klarsfeld are responsible for tracking Barbie down in Bolivia and extraditing him to France. Why do you want him brought to trial?"

Beate: "For the children of Izieu; for them alone. I don't care how Barbie treated Resistance people. They were adults—soldiers! They knew the risk. But Georgy Halpern and the others at Izieu were innocent children. Their fate was atrocious! I have two children of my own. How I wish I could do something for the Halperns! They're consumed with guilt for bringing Georgy from Zurich to France. I broke in on them with a French TV crew. They sat on their sofa, speaking only of their guilt, then they sent us away. Next morning, I sent Mrs. Halpern a dozen roses."

Hotel Cour des Loges
Lyon
10 May 1987

The Barbie trial starts tomorrow. I'm working with Marc Riboud. In our taxi from the city room of *Lyon Liberation,* where he picked up extra film, Marc made friends with the driver. Both are proud Lyonnaise. The driver said, "Barbie's trial is a mistake for Lyon and France."

Marc translated the rest: "Papa was a Resistant. In the winter of '43 he was denounced to the Gestapo by a pharmacist on the rue Volney. The pharmacist was a 'collabo' [F. slang: "collaborator"]. Papa was sent to Mauthausen concentration camp, where he worked in the quarry. He came back crippled and died at fifty-four. The pharmacist retired at sixty-five. He lives in a villa near Vienne.

"Why rake up the past? What good does it do? The proverb says, 'Le meilleur des livres est celui que l'on ouvre jamais.' ('The best of all books is the book which is never opened.')"

Ate dinner with Marc at La Belle Epoque on rue Palais-de-Justice, adjacent to the courthouse, which is under guard. National Police wearing black leather coats stroll the cobblestones.

He said, "I have a friend in Lyon whose three sons were betrayed to the Gestapo by a smuggler who promised for a fee to get them across the Spanish border. The boys, who wanted to join the Free French in Algeria, were tortured and shot. A couple of weeks after the war ended, their father learned that the smuggler had been caught. He was being held in Perpignan, under sentence of death, for denouncing the three boys. The father went there the next day and spoke with the judges. They let him command the eight-man firing squad."

11 May 1987
10:30 A.M.

That photo taken of the children at Izieu, which includes Georgy, is on page 5 of today's Paris *Trib:* Barbie is accused of murdering these children, etc.

12:30 P.M.

Outside 25 quai Romain Rolland, on the banks of the Saône, next to the Palais de Justice. My press ID tag, clipped to my lapel, is orange; Marc's, for photographers, is green; white identifies civil plaintiffs against Barbie. About forty of them, in their sixties and seventies, load Beate Klarsfeld down with bouquets of pink and red roses wrapped in cellophane. She leaves the flowers on the courthouse steps, to the left, below the row of marble Corinthian columns. The Palais de Justice now reminds me of a mausoleum.

1 P.M.

The courtroom. Enter Barbie, handcuffed; an old man. He needs a haircut in back. Did Georgy see his face that morning at Izieu?

8 P.M.

Marc (on phone from lab of *Lyon Liberation*, where he's processing photos from the trial): "Barbie's face is split in two; the halves are different. The right side sags. His smile shook me. We might have met forty-four years ago at the Hotel Terminus."

We talked more over a grilled steak at La Belle Epoque.

Marc said, "I joined the Resistance in Lyon in 1943. Earlier that year, a Father-Jesuit priest and I identified the body of my friend Jacques Molle, a Resistant, who had been tortured and shot by Miliciens [French fascists working for the Gestapo]. They burned off his feet with an acetylene torch. But he didn't betray the others in his group. I don't know if I'm that strong. I worried about betraying my friends under torture."

12 May 1987
Noon

Marc's photo of Barbie and Vergès is all over the front page of the tabloid *Lyon Liberation*. Barbie's lawyer, Jacques Vergès, in the foreground, wears thick round glasses over his Indochinese eyes. Barbie is a handsome old man.

3 P.M.

I sit in court next to Ted Morgan, who's taking notes for a book about occupied Lyon. He says, "There were so many informers here during the war that Barbie opened a special office on the place Bellecourt to handle all the denunciations."

13 May 1987

Barbie testified that, after the war, American intelligence (CIC) forced him to work by holding hostage Klaus-Georg, his infant son. His voice broke while saying, "Mein gestorbener Junge" ("My dead boy"). He took a deep breath.

An hour later, he said, "I consider myself a hostage, not a prisoner," and left the court. He sent a statement, via Vergès: "I refuse to attend the trial, having been illegally kidnaped to be taken to France."

4:14 P.M.

Rain again. Under an umbrella, on the quai Romain Rolland, a young free-lance Spanish journalist told me, "Don't feel sorry for Barbie. His son was a big shot in the neo-Nazi party called the Spanish Circle of Friends of Europe when he lived in Spain."

7:30 P.M.

Each twilight, for about an hour, swallows swoop above the wet, narrow streets around the Palais de Justice. Their cries this evening echoed outside my hotel in the rue du Boeuf.

25 quai Romain Rolland
14 May 1987
10:20 A.M.

The "Comité de Coordination de Communautés et Organisations Juives de Lyon" ("Coordinating Committee of Jewish Organizations of Lyon"). Two young guards at the door check my credentials and search my bag. I'm admitted to Serge Klarsfeld's office. He's the lawyer representing the relatives of the children of Izieu.

He says, "Forgive the guards. We get threats."

He also says, "So Dr. Halpern knows Lucien Bourdon denounced the kids to Barbie! Did Dr. Halpern tell you why? A farm! Bourdon was from Lorraine. The Germans confiscated his farm. He got it back by working for the Gestapo. He's eighty-five years old; still in Lorraine. We know where he lives. But French law prohibits us from subpoenaing him to appear in court."

Then he says, "It's likely Georgy and the other children from Izieu were thrown alive into a pit of burning corpses."

1 P.M.

On the courthouse steps, beside the wilted roses, wrapped in cellophane, is a bunch of fresh, white lilies. I should have sent Mrs. Halpern flowers.

Despite Barbie's absence from the court, a crowd at the bottom of the steps waits in the rain to be admitted.

6 P.M.

Marc takes me along for his first meeting in years with his friend Lucien Fraisse, SJ, "a Father-Jesuit," who once taught Philosophy, Theology, and Holy Scripture in Chicago.

We arrive at his apartment in the working-class rue Bossuet. Two rooms: shelves crammed with books, a copy of Rublev's icon "The Trinity" framed on the wall facing his desk. Father Fraisse was Marc's teacher in Lyon. Unbeknown to each other, they joined the Resistance. Both fought in the Vercors—the plateau near Grenoble—during the doomed Maquis uprising in July–August 1944.

Marc reminisces about the war; it gets dark. Father Fraisse, behind his desk, forgets to turn on the lights. He listens almost two hours; at one point, he covers his lap with a plaid rug.

Marc: "In April 1943, I was at a Mass in the chapel of the Maison des Etudiants Catholiques when the Father-Jesuit asked us to pray for the Jews. Many students in the shadows at the back whistled and stamped their feet. He said again, 'Let us pray for the unfortunate Jews.' The whistling got louder. Were you that priest, Father?"

"Alas, no!"

Father Fraisse served as an FFI officer in the Vercors against Waffen SS Alpine troops, then with a French Alpine Division on the Italian front. He says, "Hitler was the Anti-Christ to me. There's a close connection between Satan and National Socialism. I fought fascism since 1933. One day, in late 1943, my father came home splashed with blood. A man had thrown himself to death at his feet from the fourth floor of the new Gestapo headquarters on the place Bellecour. I joined the Resistance."

I asked, "Father, did you ever wonder: What's happening to all the Jewish men, women, and children? Did you guess they were being murdered?"

"I didn't think about them."

10 P.M.

Marc and I splurge at dinner on a bottle of Chateauneuf du Pape 1983. He orders the waiter to serve bread with the wine, then cleans his palate with one bite before taking a sip. He says, "In January, Catherine and I were on a cruise in the Caribbean with a cousin of mine and his wife who live in Lyon. They're very Catholic. We spoke about our kids. Their two sons, aged twenty and twenty-two, were staying in their apartment on the quai Tilsit. When they got home and unlocked the door, they found the apartment filled with gas. The boys were dead. They died from a leak in a broken valve on the kitchen gas heater. At the funeral, their mother said to the priest, 'Je suis dans l'enfer, mon Père.' ('I'm in hell, Father.')"

15 May 1987
Friday

En route to Paris via the 5 P.M. express train (TGV) from Perrache station, Lyon. Georgy was deported Lyon-Paris-Drancy on a passenger train. Trains to Paris cross a bridge over the Saône, which runs among poplars, then goes through a tunnel under the green hill west of Lyon called Fourviere. Georgy might have seen that stone barn with the red-tile roof.

Paris
16 May 1987

Sunny all day. "Morte aux Juifs!" ("Death to the Jews!") painted in white, with a large swastika, on a wall at the corner of rue de Vaugirard and boulevard St.-Michel.

12 rue Ste.-Catherine, Lyon
18 May 1987

With Marc, who's shooting pictures of the "traboule," marked by a wall plaque, where Barbie and his Gestapo agents grabbed eighty-six Jews on 9 February 1943. "Traboule": Lyonnaise word for characteristic local alley, open at both ends, which cuts through a building in the middle of a block. This one connects the narrow, dark rue Ste.-Catherine, stinking of piss, with the place des Terreaux, the sunlit square on which the Hotel de Ville is located. We climb the stairs; the stink gets worse. The office of the Jewish Welfare Organization, which was on the second floor, is now the Sauna Club des Terreaux: "Sauna/Relaxation/Video." Its tiny anteroom, suffused with red light, has a mirrored ceiling.

25 quai Romain Rolland
Office of Coordinating Committee
of Jewish Organizations of Lyon
3 P.M.

Mme. Aimée Meyer, née Wildman, is one of the Jewish volunteers working here. She, her mother, and her sisters were hidden during the war by villagers in Brosse, outside Lyon.

"My parents come from Poland. They got French nationality in 1932. My sisters and I were born here. The French considered us French because we spoke the language perfectly. Ordinary people saved our lives.

"Barbie caught Mother's nephew, Alex, in the summer of 1944. Alex was fifteen. He and his mother were hiding with their Christian friends in Lyon. Alex, who was gifted in mathematics, didn't want to fall behind in his studies, so he secretly took lessons from his former math teacher at the man's apartment on the rue Vendôme. I forget his name. He and his wife were in the Resistance.

"Late one afternoon, Barbie arrested them all in the apartment. He slapped Alex twice, then said in French, 'I smell a Jew!' Alex denied it. Barbie made him pull down his pants. Alex remembers staring at Barbie's leather whip; he tapped his whip against the heel of one shoe. Alex was taken to 'the Jew barrack' at Fort Montluc. After a month, he was sent to Drancy. Then he was deported to Germany. The train en route slowed down because of an air-raid alarm. Alex jumped off.

"He told the two railway workers who found him, 'I'm a Jew who's escaped from the Germans.' They saved his life. The mathematics teacher and his wife never came back."

5 P.M.

François, the bartender at my hotel, tells me he read in *Lyon Liberation* that Barbie trained his German shepherd dog to bite the genitals off naked prisoners. He said, "Barbie is old. My good parents are dead. God is not fair."

The place Neuve St.-Jean
9:30 P.M.

A bare-chested fire-eater rinses his mouth from a wine bottle filled with some flammable fluid, then blows across a lighted taper in his right hand. A 6-foot-long fire whooshes from his mouth above a motorcycle parked in the cobblestones. A young waiter from the restaurant opposite runs across the street and moves the bike. A pretty redhead laughs.

19 May 1987

Lyon Liberation reports the following: On Saturday night a mass dedicated to the memory of French volunteers in the

Waffen SS, who were killed fighting for Hitler on the eastern front, was celebrated at the church of Ste. Irenée, on the rue Marseilles. The service was organized by a local neo-Nazi organization called the CLAN (the Lyon Committee of National Action).

1 P.M.

Marc makes friends with M. Boucard, the new manager of the Hotel Terminus, opposite the north entrance of the Perrache railroad station.

Boucard tells him that in March, a seventy-eight-year-old lady rented Room 521 for one night. She said, "Barbie m'a y torturé à la baignoire" ("Barbie tortured me there in the bathtub").

In April, because of the upcoming trial, Boucard decided to renovate the whole fifth floor. He also bricked up the entrance to the tunnel, dug by the Gestapo, between the hotel's wine cellar and Perrache station, through which prisoners were taken to the trains.

Barbie and his fellow Gestapo and SS officers drank the cellar dry. They got drunk in the lobby, under a painting of locomotives and half-naked nymphs, wreathed in smoke, called, "The Allegory of the Railroads."

Going up in the elevator, Marc spots a swastika scratched on the corrugated aluminum wall; I point out two more cut into the top of the brass frame holding a hotel menu under glass: "Gratinée Lyonnaise . . . 25 F." We count fifty others, along with the word "Heil!" Put here when?

The fifth floor smells of fresh paint. Brushes, paint cans, a spattered tarp over a wooden chair. In one of the sunny rooms on my right, a tenor is singing the Christmas carol "Gloria in Excelsis Deo." Marc explains that French house painters always sing while they work. "They're famous for their sweet voices."

Room 521 has just been plastered. The new tub in the bathroom is to the left of the low, opened window that overlooks the roof of the station and a church steeple.

Marc: "I read that Barbie kept the shutters closed."

3 P.M.

On a wall, near the Palais de Justice: "C'est l'enfer, l'éternelle peine!" ("This is hell, eternal punishment!") —Rimbaud.

Underneath, in a different hand: "Il y a plus qu'un Enfer!"—Dieu. ("There is more than one hell!" —God.)

3:30 P.M.

Richard Bernstein, Paris Bureau Chief, *New York Times,* learned over lunch that I covered the Eichmann trial in Jerusalem, 1961. He wants to know my feelings: "What's the difference between then and now?"

"During the Eichmann trial, I was twenty-eight and unmarried. The murder of kids didn't affect me much. That's all I think about here."

5:30 P.M.

Father Fraisse: "Our generation has experienced the truth about history: evil is real. The human condition hasn't changed since Adam and Eve. The world awaits its Redeemer. Nothing about the war—not even the murder of children—shakes my faith."

I said, "It cost me mine."

20 May 1987
7 P.M.

With Marc at Izieu. Georgy is listed on the plaque as 'Georges Halperm, 9 Ans.' Standing beneath Mme. Thibaudier's potted begonias is a wreath of plastic red roses, with a purple ribbon, inscribed "Auschwitz" in gold letters.

M. Perret, the mayor of Izieu, invites us home for a whiskey. He's in his seventies, a widower for nine years. During the war, he often came to visit his parents in Izieu. They—everyone here —knew about the Jewish children hiding in the big white house. M. Perret saw them around town. He remembers two little girls picking red carnations near the church. He can't recall Georgy.

In court
21 May 1987

Michel Thomas escaped from Barbie on the rue Ste.-Catherine in February 1943. My French gave out during his testimony. Spoke English outside with Marek Halter, Jewish-French novelist, who survived the Warsaw Ghetto. I asked him, "Why hold this trial after forty-three years?"

"Forty years is the right amount of time! It counts in the Bible as a generation. Think how long the children of Israel wandered in the desert. This is probably the last public trial of a Nazi. The Holocaust generation is getting old. We wander in the wilderness. It takes forty years for memories to pass into history and myth. That's what's happening here. This is our last chance to set the record straight."

22 May 1987

Breakfast at the hotel with Michel Thomas, who owns a language school in New York. He said, "My command of languages —and knowing when to shut up—saved my life on February 9, 1943. I fooled Barbie into letting me go from the roundup of Jews on the rue Ste.-Catherine. I went there that morning in my capacity as an officer in the Resistance to persuade my fellow Jews at the Welfare Organization to support our fight. I went disguised as a French artist. I carried with me as cover a portfolio of twenty-five of my own watercolor landscapes.

"Soon as I opened that door on the second floor, a Gestapo officer grabbed my neck with both hands, and yelled, 'Kommen Sie 'rein!' 'Come inside!' I couldn't let on that I understood German. I was born in Poland but educated in Germany and France. Only Jews in Lyon knew German; the language often gave them away.

"I said in French, 'I don't understand what you want, monsieur,' and told a long story, which I made up on the spot, about being here to sell a painting to a Jew named M. Pollack.

"Two Gestapo officers, wearing black uniforms, took me into the next room, in front of a man seated behind a table. The officer on my left drew his pistol and cocked it. I heard the click. He said to the others in German, 'Let's finish this Jew off. I'll shoot him in the ear.' I didn't turn a hair. I jabbered away in my best French: the most idiomatic.

"The man behind the table wore a suit and tie. He had blue-gray eyes; the halves of his face didn't match. His right ear was lower than his left. He questioned me in French for an hour and a half. It was so cold I saw his breath. I became aware that behind me the room was crowded with Jews—old men, young women, kids. Out of the corner of my eye, I saw a little boy with his hands in the air.

"I realized that facing me across the table was the 'Malech Hamavis'—in Yiddish, the Angel of Death. I spread out my false papers. He looked them over.

"How I talked! 'I'm a struggling artist! French! What does monsieur want? I don't understand!' etc. etc. I made myself sound irritated, not scared. Once he jumped up and screamed at me in German, 'You dirty Jew!' I looked blank. I was surprised how short he was. I thought, 'I'm a dead man if he makes me pull down my pants!'

"He let me go at noon. I escaped the Angel of Death."

26 May 1987

Barbie's enforced return to court brought back to Lyon lots of journalists, including an ABC-TV sound man, who told me the following:

Q.: "What's a Barbie-Q?"
A.: "The new German microwave oven that seats twelve."

When the court let out this evening, Marc photographed Vergès on the steps of the Palais de Justice. I caught the gist of their conversation. Vergès asked how does France dare prosecute Barbie? The French tortured and murdered more Algerians, proportionate to the Algerian population, than the Germans tortured and murdered here.

Marc's reply was interrupted by a man who shook Vergès's hand, and said, "Bravo, M. Vergès, vous faites du bon travail! Continuez!" ("Congratulations, Mr. Vergès! Keep up the good work!")

Marc and I went to Fort Montluc, the military prison where Georgy and the others had been locked in the "Jew barracks" for one week. The prison is still used by the French army. Georgy was admitted through a steel door with a grille over the window.

We looked down at the walled yard from the fifth floor balcony of an apartment building on the rue Dauphine. The former "Jew barracks" is the single-story cell block, with a red-tile roof. Its tall windows are barred. Georgy probably saw the tops of those acacia trees beyond the walls. What would he make of the jet trail in the eastern sky?

Marc: "Ex-prisoners from the 'Jew barracks' say there was no plumbing. The place stank. Walls and ceilings crawled with roaches, worms, and lice. They dropped on the prisoners all night."

> 26 May 1987
>
> Dear Marilyn,
>
> Georgy's trail is cold. I'm reduced to conjecturing what he might have experienced. Maybe the witnesses who testify tomorrow will remember him.

Office of Coordinating Committee
27 May 1987
11:30 A.M.

Mme. Sabina Zlatin arrived with Mme. Lea Feldblum and Leon Reifmann, the adults who survived the raid on the house at Izieu. They will testify in court today.

Mme. Feldblum came from Israel; a number is tattooed on her left forearm. She and Mme. Zlatin hadn't seen each other in forty-three years.

Dr. Reifmann said he can't remember Georgy. Neither can Mme. Feldblum, whose lower lip trembled. She broke into Yiddish, which I partly followed: "I loved Emile Zuckerberg best at Izieu. He was taken from my arms on the platform at Birkenau."

Mme. Zlatin doesn't remember Georgy either; the 200 francs he needed for shoes doesn't ring a bell. Her husband, Miron, looked after the children's shoes. He was shot on 31 July 1944. "I can no longer remember any one child in particular. Too much time has passed."

She said, "I blame myself for choosing that house at Izieu. Marcel Wiltzer, the local subprefecture of police, who was a Resistant, showed me several houses before the one at Izieu. I chose it because he said, 'Izieu will be tranquil.' "

29 May 1987

At Izieu all afternoon with Marc. Mme. Thibaudier was widowed last summer. She shows us her walled garden behind the house, which was built by a rich bourgeois around the turn of the century. The water in the concrete pool where Georgy swam is covered with algae. There are buds on the rosebushes.

We watch the 1 P.M. news on TV in Mme. Thibaudier's kitchen. She and her husband bought this house in 1950; no one had lived here since that April morning in 1944. "I've kept some of the children's things in the attic where they studied. There's a little cardboard suitcase, school desks, mattresses, some pictures on the walls."

The dusty attic is dark. We make out five photos, cut from magazines, pasted on a whitewashed wall near the floor. I light a match; we see faded mountains, a horse, a cow, a blond woman holding a blond child in her arms.

Marc pulls a rotten board off the oeil-de-boeuf window in the next room. It stays dark. One mattress lies rolled-up on a narrow bench; another hangs by a cord from a nail in the low ceiling. The cardboard suitcase is empty. Marc discovers two papers pasted inside the tops of two old-fashioned school desks. By the light of a match, I read the one on the left: a calendar written in a school-boy's hand for the week beginning Sunday, 16 March 1944.

The other, written in the same hand: a schedule of daily classes. Georgy took arithmetic from 8:30 to 9:30 A.M.

Marc speaks with Julien Favet while he waters his tomatoes. M. Favet is the sixty-eight-year-old retired hired hand who testified the day before in court that he saw Barbie here on Thursday morning, 6 April 1944. "I looked into his blue eyes."

He said, "I worked that morning in the vineyard till about nine-thirty." On his way back for breakfast, he was stopped on the road, under a linden tree, by a German sentry with a submachine gun. Two trucks were parked outside the white house. Two soldiers questioned him.

"I played the fool."

The German in command wore a suit and tie. "He listened to my imbecilic replies, then said in French, 'You can go!'

"That's when I looked into his eyes.

"The German soldiers beat the children with rifle butts, yelling, 'Schnell! Schnell!' and loaded them on the trucks. One little boy jumped off. Two soldiers threw him back like a sack of potatoes.

"Another little boy I knew cried out to me, 'Julien, help us!' The fifteen-year-old—I forget his name—said, 'Julien, c'est la fin pour nous!' ('Julien, this is the end for us!')

"Every night for a week afterward I was awakened by this dream: a child stands before me. I can't recognize his face. He wasn't from Izieu. I knew those children. We were friends. They called me Julien. Tell me, messieurs: who was that child in my dreams?"